Financial Markets Management
Class XI

by

Harsha Jarani

Financial Markets Management
Class XI
by Harsha Jarani

ISBN: 978-93-62760-93-7

Published by

DOUBLE 9 BOOKS

2/13-B, Ansari Road
Daryaganj, New Delhi – 110002
info@double9books.com
www.double9books.com
Tel. 011-40042856

ABOUT THE AUTHOR

I am highly elated to pen down this book with the aim to foster and imbibe current directional methodological approach that can be fulfilling the recent demands of acquiring the knowledge related Financial Markets Management. Future Perspective of this subject are highly in demand to meet the existing market competition. This book has been systematically crafted to provide crystal clear analytical understanding of the facts and figures associated with the subject and to be students friendly . I'm having keen interest in this subject therefore, it interests me to put forth 180-degree crystal clear information, interpretation, comprehension, analysis and understanding based contents that may fulfil the demand of youngsters of 21st century. I am highly elated with the publication of the First edition of this book. I am sure that it will be able to meet the current demands of aspiring students. I am Ms. Harsha Jarani, has written this book (Financial Markets management) for STD XI CBSE Board. I have been striving hard to bring easy solutions with the publication of this reference book looking at the least number of resources available for the subject in the market.

CONTENTS

Preface

This book is written on the basics of financial Markets. As we know very little about the share and other stocks . This book will help the students to understand the basic things about the **Financial Market** like the **National Stock Exchange.** It is written on the basis of NSE pdf available in cbse website. This book includes detailed basic knowledge of financial marketing.

The Features of this book are

a) Numerous worked Example to illustrate the concept

b) Detailed explanation of each and every topic

c) Numerous Question For Practice (MCQ) after each and every unit

d) Sample papers along with answer

I hope this book will help the students to learn Financial Marketing in a more clear way and increase their curiosity to acquire knowledge about the investment and its process.

Acknowledgement

This book is based on the syllabus of Financial Markets Management of CBSE class XI commerce.

I would like to thank my friends and colleagues for encouraging me to start the work, preserve it and finally to publish it.

I would like to thank Double9 publication for helping me to publish this book. Finally I would like to acknowledge my gratitude, the support, and love my family My Husband , Anil: My son Manan: they all kept me going, this book would not have been possible without them

- NSE- National Stock Exchange of India Ltd.
- SEBI - Securities Exchange Board of India
- NCFM - NSE's Certification in Financial Markets
- NSDL - National Securities Depository Limited
- CSDL - Central Depository Services (India) Limited
- NCDEX - National Commodity and Derivatives Exchange Ltd.
- NSCCL - National Securities Clearing Corporation Ltd.
- FMC - Forward Markets Commission
- NYSE- New York Stock Exchange
- AMEX - American Stock Exchange
- OTC- Over-the-Counter Market LM - Lead Manager
- IPO- Initial Public Offer DP - Depository Participant
- DRF - Demat Request Form
- RRF - Remat Request Form
- NAV - Net Asset Value EPS - Earnings Per Share
- DSCR - Debt Service Coverage Ratio
- IISL - India Index Services & Products Ltd
- CRISIL- Credit Rating Information Services of India Limited
- CARE - Credit Analysis & Research Limited
- ICRA - Investment Information and Credit Rating Agency of India
- ISC - Investor Service Cell IPF - Investor Protection Fund
- SCRA - Securities Contract (Regulation) Act
- SCRR - Securities Contract (Regulation) Rules
- NSC – National Savings Certificate
- PPF – Public Provident Fund
- MCX – Multi Commodity Exchange of India
- NCDEX – National Commodities and Derivatives Exchange

- DP – Depository Participant DEA – Department of Economic Affairs
- DCA - Department of Company Affairs
- ETF – Exchange Traded Funds
- IPO – Initial Public Offering
- NAV – Net Asset Value
- ROC – Registrar of Companies
- ASBA – Applications Supported by Blocked Amounts
- GDR – Global Depository Receipts
- ADR – American Depository Receipts
- FCCB – Foreign Currency Convertible Bonds
- SCORES – SEBI Complaint Redressal System
- ADS – American Depositary Share
- NEAT – National Exchange for Automated Trading
- NYSE – New York Stock Exchange
- NASDAQ - National Association of Securities Dealers Automated Quotation System
- AMEX – American Stock Exchange
- OTC – Over the Counter
- SBTS – Screen Based Trading system

Unit 1
Markets and Financial Instruments

Introduction:-

Before proceeding with the topic each and everybody should know about financial market

Financial Market

A Financial Market is referred to space, where selling and buying of financial assets and securities take place. It allocates limited resources in the nation's economy. It serves as an agent between the investors and collector by mobilising capital between them

Financial Instruments

In simple words, any asset which holds capital and can be traded in the market is referred to as a financial instrument. Some examples of financial instruments are cheques, shares, stocks, bonds, futures, and options contracts.

In financial market most of investor do the investment so we need to learn the terms first:-

1) What is the investment

The money you earn is partly spent and the rest of the amount is saved for meeting future expenses. Instead of keeping the savings idle you may like to use savings in order to get returns on it in the future. This is called Investment.

OR

Investment refers to putting your money in an asset with the aim of generating income. Financial investments come in different forms, such as mutual funds, unit linked investment plans, endowment plans, stocks, bonds and more.

2) Benefits of investment (Why should one invest)

- a) Earn return on your idle resources
- b) Generate a specified sum of money for a specific goal in life
- c) Make a provision for an uncertain future
- d) One of the important reasons why one needs to invest wisely is to meet the cost of Inflation

(Cost of inflation :-Inflation causes money to lose value because it will not buy the same amount of a good or a service in the future as it does now or did in the past.)

3) Aim of investment

The aim of investments should be to provide a return above the inflation rate to ensure that the investment does not decrease in value. **For example, if the annual inflation rate is 6%, then the investment will need to earn more than 6% to ensure it increases in value.** Otherwise your asset will decrease in value

Return > rate of inflation otherwise it will lead to loss for investor

4) When to start investing

Golden rule of investment

- a) Invest early
- b) Invest regularly
- c) Invest for long term and not short term

By investing early you will give chance to your investment to grow compoundly and thereby increase your income

5) What care should be taken while investing

Before making any investment you should ensure the following details

- a) Obtain the written document
- b) Check the legitimacy of the documents (whether that document is fake or genuine)
- c) Read the instruction in document carefully
- d) Find out the cost and return of the securities in which you are investing (cost of investment like brokerage cost, market analysis cost etc should be less than the return you will get in future)

e) Check the risk you are taking and return you are getting that means more risk more return should be there and vice versa

f) If the security is liquid (easily convertible in cash) are seems to be much safer as compare to risky security

g) Investment should help you to achieve your goals of investment

h) Compare the details of investment with other securities available in the market

i) Do the investment only through the registered intermediaries like broker , sub-broker that should be registered with SEBI

j) Seek necessary information about the intermediary by checking the website of SEBI (to know the intermediary are genuine or fraud)

k) Invest in any security only if you are comfortable about the securities

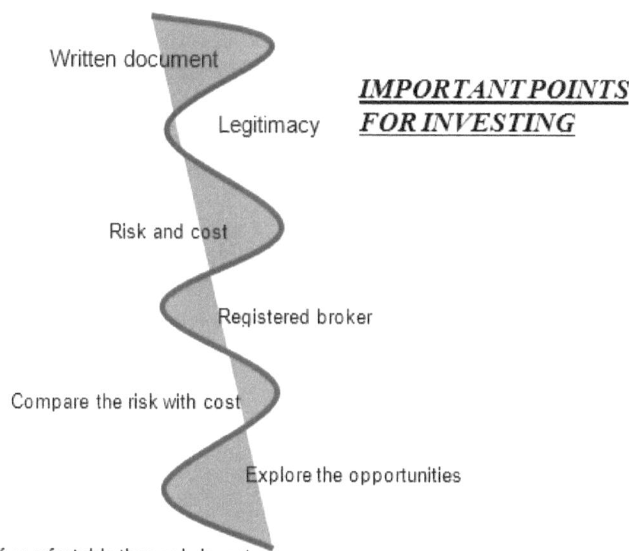

What is the return?

a) Return may be in form of interest or dividend, that we are getting by investing our money in debentures and shares respectively

b) Interest is an amount charged to the borrower for the privilege of using the lender's money.

c) Interest is usually the amount charged for using the investors money and calculated on the principal amount

What is the interest rate?

Interest rate may be of different type

a) Rate which is charged by bank on loan borrowed

b) Rate on which bank pay interest to saving and fixed deposit holder

c) Rate at which government will pay to investor on bonds like state and central government bonds

Factors determine the interest rate

a) Demand for money

b) Supply of money to

c) Rate of inflation

d) Level of government borrowings (Government may subscribe for bonds to public and accordingly the level of borrowing will increase and vice versa)

The few of above policies are decided by RBI and Government of India

Various option available for investment

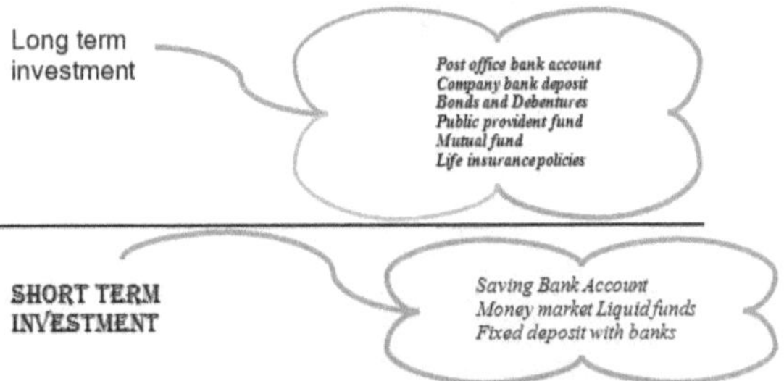

Long term investment

A long-term investment is an account a company plans to keep for at least a year such as stocks, bonds, real estate etc.

Types of long term investment

1) **Post office saving:-** It is a type of instrument that invests investors money in the post office.

a) It provides interest rate of **8.4%**

b) Minimum amount, which can be invested, is Rs. ***1,000/-*** and additional investment in multiples of 1,500/-.

c) Maximum amount is Rs. ***4,50,000/-*** (if Single) or Rs. ***9,00,000/- (if held Jointly)*** during a year. It has a maturity period of 6 years.

d) A bonus of 10% is paid at the time of maturity..

e) Deduction can done if investor withdraw \money before the date of maturity (deduction is up-to 5% will be done and 10% bonus will be automatically cancelled)

2) Public Provident Fund:-

PPF is having the interest rate of 8.7% p.a and having the maturity period of 15 years

Opened through the nationalised bank only

According to PPF partial withdrawal rules, you can withdraw up to 50 percent of the amount in your PPF Account after seven years, starting from the end of the year you made your first contribution. You can make only one partial withdrawal each year.

Advantages of PPF

a) Tax benefits: PPF offers tax benefits on both returns and investments. Contributions up to INR 1.5 lakh per year are tax-free under Section 80C. Withdrawals and returns are also tax-free.

b) Low risk: PPF is a low-risk investment with guaranteed returns.

c) Investment flexibility: PPF offers investment flexibility.

d) Tax-free interest income: PPF offers tax-free interest income.

Disadvantages of PPF

a) PPF has a 15-year lock-in period, longer than some other tax-saving options. This makes it less flexible in case of any emergency situation.

b) Moderate Interest Rate: PPF offers relatively lower interest rates compared to other long-term investments, like ULIP, Capital Guarantee Plans, and ELSS.

3) <u>Company Fixed deposit</u>

    a) The company FD may be of long term, short term or moderate term. The company fixed deposit pay fixed rate of interest which may varies between 8 to 12%

    b) There is also a cumulative fixed deposit(whole deposit at the end of maturity) where the whole amount is paid along with principal and interest at the end of the loan period. The interest is paid generally after deduction of tax.

> *Note:-(As corporate FDs are unsecured and are typically not backed by collateral, they carry higher risks than bank FDs. While banks and NBFCs are well regulated by the Reserve Bank of India (RBI), which reviews their performance regularly, there is no such regulator for company FD; these are governed by the company law.)*

4) <u>Bonds and debentures:-</u>

Bonds are generally instrument issued to pay certain sum of money at the time of maturity issued by central and state government

Dentures are similar type of instrument issued by company, generally in the form of convertible non-convertible bonds bearing fixed rate of interest

    a) Convertible debentures are converted into equity shares at the option of holder at the time of maturity only

    b) Non- convertible debentures are pais fully to the holder at the time maturity

    c) Partly convertible debentures are fully paid on maturity and partly converted into maturity and partly fully paid at the time of maturity

5) <u>Mutual Funds:-</u>

Mutual funds let you pool your money with other investors to "mutually" buy stocks, bonds, and other investments. They're run by professional money managers who decide which securities to buy (stocks, bonds, etc.) and when to sell them.

It is substitute for those who unable to invest in equities or debentures because of time or knowledge constraints

Benefits of Mutual Fund

- Managed professionally by professionals
- You can buy units of mutual funds in small amount and diversify your investment

- Mutual funds units are redeemed by FUND MANAGEMENT COMPANY based on the NAV

NAV= $\dfrac{\text{Value of all units} - \text{expenses}}{\text{No of units}}$

- Mutual funds are generally long term investment funds, though some categories of mutual funds are dealt in money market

6) *Life insurance policies:-*

A life insurance policy is a legally binding contract between an insurance company and a policyholder.

The insurance company provides financial protection to the policyholder and pays a death benefit to the nominee when the insured dies.

It is a good method to protect your family financially, in case of death, by providing funds for the loss of income.

- *Types of policies are Endowment policies, annuities policies, unit linked plan*

  a) *Endowment policy:-* periodic payment of premiums and a lump sum amount either in the event of death of the insured or on the date of expiry of the policy, whichever occurs earlier

  b) *Annuities/pension policies:-* It give a guaranteed income for life or for a certain period. In case of the death, or after the fixed annuity period expires for annuity payments, the invested annuity fund is refunded, usually with some additional amounts as per the terms of the policy.

  c) *Unit Linked insurance plan:-* A ULIP is an insurance plan that offers the dual benefit of investment to fulfil your long-term goals, and a life cover` to financially protect your family in case of an unfortunate event.

Types of Short term assets

a) Money Market or Liquid Funds:-

These are a specialised form of mutual funds that invest in extremely short-term fixed income instruments and thereby provide easy liquidity. Money market mutual funds are protecting your capital and give easy returns. Money market funds usually yield better returns than savings accounts, but lower than bank fixed deposits.

b) Saving bank account

A savings account is a safe investment option that allows you to earn interest on your deposited amount. Normally it allows the interest rate up-to 4% to 6%

Types of saving bank account

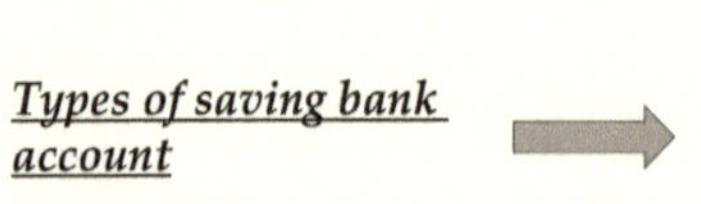

c) Fixed deposit

- A fixed deposit (FD) is a type of investment where an individual deposits a lump sum amount with a bank for a set period of time. *(6-12 months investment period as normally interest on less than 6 months)*

- The bank pays a guaranteed interest rate on the deposit for the agreed-upon tenure. At the end of the tenure, the depositor receives their original investment plus compound interest.

- FDs are also known as term deposits.

- They are considered one of the safest investments, but there are many different options available.

- The tenure of the FD is decided by the investor and can range from a few days to several years. However, if the depositor wants to withdraw their funds before the FD matures, they may be liable for a penalty. Banks typically charge between 0.50% and 1.00% of the interest as a penalty.

Meaning of Stock Exchange

The Securities Contract (Regulation) Act, 1956 [SCRA] defines _Stock Exchange' as any body of individuals, whether incorporated or not, constituted for the purpose of assisting, regulating or controlling the business of buying, selling or dealing in securities.

Stock exchange could be a regional stock exchange whose area of operation/jurisdiction is specified at the time of its recognition or national exchanges, which are permitted to have nationwide trading since inception. NSE was incorporated as a national stock exchange.

➡ *Equity shares*

An equity share is a company's partial ownership. It represents a unit of part ownership in the company. Equity shares are also referred to as common stock, or common shares.

 a) Investors in such shares hold the right to vote, share profits and claim assets of a company.

 b) Unlike debt instruments, equity shares do not create a fixed obligation on the company to pay dividends. The payment of dividends is subject to the discretion of the company's board of directors.

(For example, in a company the total equity capital of Rs 200,00,000 is divided into 20,00,000 units of Rs 10 each. Each such unit of Rs 10 is called a Share. Thus, the company then is said to have 20,00,000 equity shares of Rs. 10 each.)

➡ *Debt instrument*

A debt instrument is a written contract that allows organisations to raise funds. Debt instruments are assets that require a fixed payment to the holder, usually with interest

Debt instrument is of two types:-

 a) **Bonds :** these are generally issued by central, state and public sector organisations.

 b) **Debentures:** these are generally issued by private organisations.

➡ *Derivative*

The term derivative refers to a type of financial contract whose value is dependent on an underlying asset (shares, debentures, commodity, currency) or group of assets, or benchmark.

A derivative is set between two or more parties that can trade on an exchange or over-the-counter

- The financial derivatives came into the spotlight in the post-1970 period due to growing instability in the financial markets.

- However, these products have become very popular and by 1990s, they accounted for about two-thirds of total transactions in derivative products.

➡ Index

The indices are performance indicators that indicate the performance of a certain market segment or the market as a whole.

The indices help the interested investor to compare market performance of the stock with respect to benchmark stock within that sector.The main index of the NSE is the Nifty 50. The Nifty 50 is a well diversified 51 stock index accounting for 13 sectors of the economy.

It is used as a benchmark to measure the performance of the stock

➡ Depositories

A depository is a financial institution that holds and maintains securities for investors in electronic form. Depositories can include banks, credit unions, and savings and loans institutions.

Advantages of depositories

- *The transfers take place immediately unlike physical transfer. The beneficial owner also transfers as soon as the shares are transferred from one account to the other.*

- *It only holds the securities listed in a particular stock exchange.*

- *The issue of fake certificates, the problem-related to bad delivery or any kind of issue related to signature are also reduced.*

- *Now there is no need to fill a transfer form and affix share transfer form in order to transfer shares.*

- *The electronic system is time-saving.*

- *The fear of losing the certificate or issue of fraud certificates are also eliminated.*

- *Transfer of benami properties is also restricted.*

➡ Dematerialisation

Dematerialization is the process by which physical certificates of an investor are converted to an equivalent number of securities in electronic form and credited to the investor's account with his Depository Participant (DP).

India introduced the Demat Account system in 1996 for trades on NSE. Today, there's no paperwork involved, and physical certificates are no longer issued.

Importance of Dematerialisation

- An investor can manage his securities just by using a computer or a smartphone.

- Dematerialisation reduces the cost of holding share certificates.

- There is no stamp duty on electronic certificates, and the holding charges are nominal.

➡ *Share certificate*

A share certificate is a written document signed on behalf of a corporation that serves as legal proof of ownership of the number of shares indicated. A share certificate is also referred to as a stock certificate.

Importance

Share certificates serve as proof of ownership and are essential for various purposes, such as transferring ownership, raising capital, and maintaining transparency in corporate governance.

The above is the image of a physical share certificate. When this is dematerialised, it will be converted to electronic form. The physical certificate will be destroyed and the number of shares held will be transferred to the beneficiary account.

SHARE CERTIFICATE
(Incorporated under the Companies Act, 1956)

Certificate No. ______________ No. of Shares ________ Shares Ledger Folio ____________

No. of Shares ____________ from ____________ to ____________________ both inclusive

Name____

Father / Husband Name_________________________________ Occupation_____________

Address____

Given under the Common Seal of the Company this ___________ day of ______________

| Authorised Signatory | Director | Managing Director |

MEMORANDUM OF CALLS PAID

Date	Receipt	Particulars	Per Share	Amount	Signature
		Application ____________			
		Allotment ____________			
		1st Call ____________			
		2nd Call ____________			

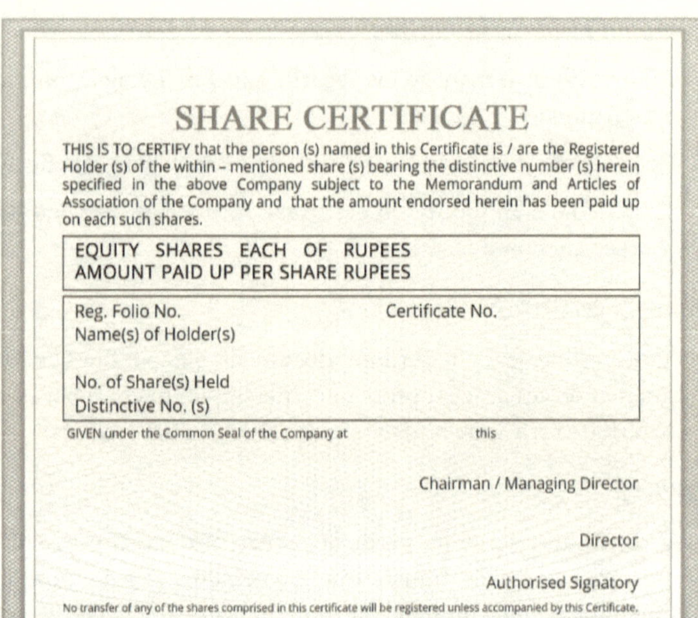

➡ *Define securities*

Securities are tradable financial assets that can be used to raise capital in public and private markets. They can also be defined as investments in a business.

There are three main types of securities:

- ***Equity:*** Provides ownership rights to holders

- ***Debt:*** Essentially loans that are repaid with periodic payments

- ***Hybrids:*** Combine aspects of debt and equity

Examples *of securities* ➡

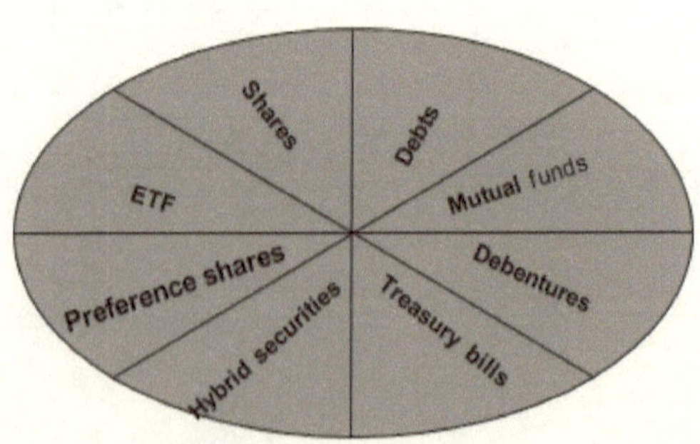

What are the functions of Securities Market

1. The primary function of the securities markets is to enable the flow of capital from those that have it, to those that need it.

2. Securities market helps in transfer of resources from those with idle resources to others who have a productive need for them.

3. It will lead to mobilising of idle resources

4. It will help entrepreneur and corporates to raise resources through public

5. Security market provides channel for reallocation of saving to investment

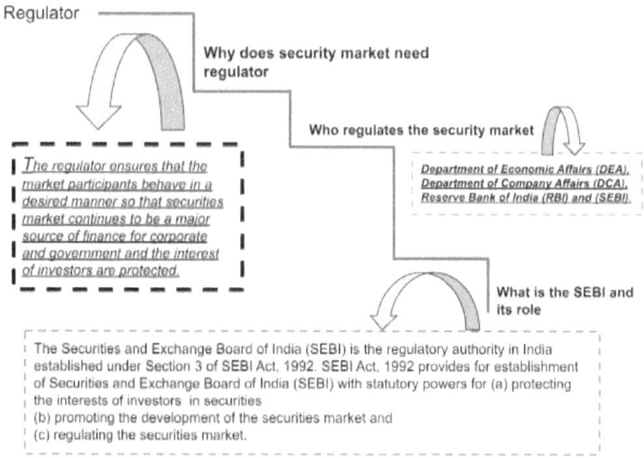

Importance of SEBI

Regulating the business in stock exchanges and any other securities markets

Registering and regulating the working of stock brokers, sub-brokers etc.

Promoting and regulating self-regulatory organizations Prohibiting fraudulent and unfair trade practices

Who *are the* participants in Securities Market

1. The securities market essentially has three categories of participants, namely, the issuers of securities(companies), investors in securities and the intermediaries, such as merchant bankers, brokers etc.

2. While the corporates and Government raise resources from the securities market to meet their obligations, it is households and

other corporates and financial institutions that invest their savings in the securities market.

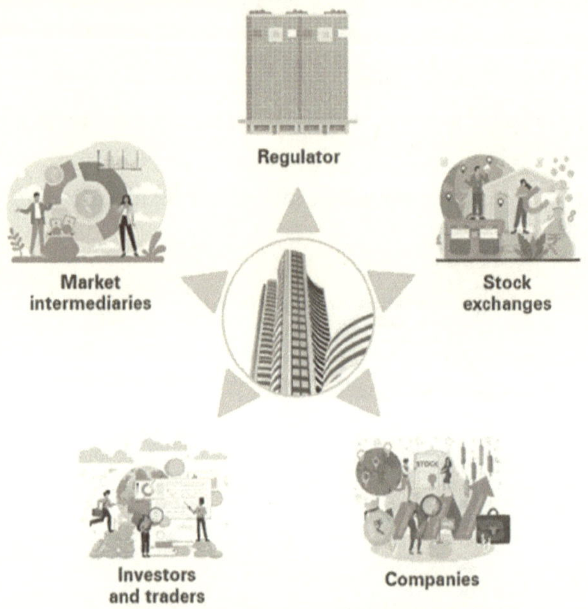

Multiple choice question

I. _____________ is often the first banking product people use, which owens low interest

a) **Saving bank account**

b) Money market or liquid fund

c) Fixed deposit with banks

d) Post office saving

II. _____________ defines stock exchange as any body of individuals whether incorporated or not

a) National stock exchange of India Ltd

b) **SEBI regulation Act 1956**

c) Government of India

d) RBI

III.   ______________ represents a contract whereby one party lends money to another on predetermined terms with regards to rate and periodicity of interest

a) Derivative

b) **Debt instrument**

c) Mutual fund

d) Index

IV.   A ________ is like a bank wherein the deposits are securities in electronic form

a) **Depositary**

b) Depository participant

c) Demat account

d) Custodian

V.   Define equity shares

VI.   ______________ is a contract providing for payment of a sum of money to the person assured of or following him to the person entitled to receive the same

a) Company fixed deposit

b) Bonds and debentures

c) Provident fund

d) **Life insurance policies**

VII.   Define bonus shares

VIII.   Which of the following statement is not true while investing

a) Obtain written documents explaining the investment

b) Read and understand such documents

c) Verify the legitimacy of the investment

d) **Don't assess the risk return profile of the investment**

IX   When we borrow money, we are expected to pay for using it - this is known as________

a) Profit

b) Return

c) **Interest**

d) Dividend

X.   minimum investment period for bank FDs is ____________

a) One year

b) 15 year

c) 90 days

d) **30 days**

XI.   ______________ is a fixed income instrument issued for a period of more than one year with the purpose of raising capital.

a) Debt

b) Share

c) Government securities

d) **Bonds and debentures**

XII   ______________ is a contract providing for payment of a sum of money to the person assured or, following him to the person entitled to receive the same, on the happening of a certain event.

a) Company fixed deposit

b) Mutual funds

c) Derivative

d) **Life insurance policy**

XIII.   ____________ is a product whose value is derived from the value of one or more basic variables, called underlying.

a) Share

b) Debentures

c) **Derivative**

d) Mutual funds

XIV   ____________shows how a specified portfolio of share prices are moving in order to give an indication of market trends.

a) **Index**

b) Stock exchange

c) Market analysis

d) Fund manager

XV.   ___________ is like a bank wherein the deposits are securities in electronic form.

a) Custodian

b) **Depositary**

c) Clearing bank

d) RTA

XVI.   ___________ is a place where buyers and sellers of securities can enter into transactions to purchase and sell shares, bonds, debentures etc.

a) Security market

b) Stock exchange

c) **Both a or b**

d) None of the above

XVII.   The absence of conditions of perfect competition in the securities markets makes the role of the ___________

a) Stock exchange

b) Broker

c) Intermediary

d) **Regulatory authority**

XVIII.   The regulator ensures that the ___________ behave in a desired manner

a) **Market participant**

b) Investor

c) Broker

d) Intermediary

XIX.   ___________ regulates the Securities Market

a) Department of Economic Affairs (DEA),

b) Department of Company Affairs (DCA),

c) Reserve Bank of India (RBI) and Securities and Exchange Board of India (SEBI)

d) **All of the above**

XX. What are the golden rules for investors?

a) Invest early

b) Invest regularly

c) Invest in long term and not short term

d) **All of the above**

XXI What care should an investor take while investing?

a) Verify the legitimacy of the investment

b) Ascertain if it is appropriate for your specific goals

c) Examine if it fits in with other investments you are considering or you have already made

d) **All of the above**

XXII What are the factors that determine Interest Rate?

a) Demand for Money

b) Supply of Money

c) Deflation rate

d) **All of the above**

XXIII What type of asset are the Commodities are considered?

a) Physical Asset

b) Financial Asset

c) Both a & b

d) **None of the above**

XXIV Which of these is a Long-Term Investment?

a) Money Market Funds

b) **Public Provident Fund**

c) Both nand b

d) None of the above

XXV. Which of these are powers of SEBI?

a) Regulating the business in stock exchanges and any other securities markets

b) Promoting and regulating self-regulatory organisations

c) Prohibiting fraudulent and unfair trade practices

d) **All of the above**

<u>*Define the following*</u>

1. Share
2. Dematerialisation
3. Stock exchange
4. Dematerialisation
5. Debt instrument
6. Interest
7. Depositary
8. Mutual fund
9. Derivative

<u>*Write short question*</u>

1. When to start investing ?
2. What factors determine interest rate ?
3. What are the options available for investment?
4. What is the function of the securities market ?
5. Why does the security market need a regulator ?
6. Who are the participants of the securities market?
7. What are the segments of the security market ?
8. What is the difference between short and long term investment
9. Difference between Depository and Bank
10. Explain the difference between bonds and debentures
11. Explain any two long term investment

<u>*Long questions (Write the answer in 50-80 words each)*</u>

1. In an economy like India, if there is a change in taxation policy of the government related to income,is it going to affect the interest rate in the market also? Justify your answer
2. Being as an investor you have conducted the market analysis of the investment in which you want to invest then also , is it necessary for you to appoint the intermediary for dealing in shares ? Justify your answer
3. SEBI is the regulator of the stock market. According to you , is it necessary to have the regulator in the market

4. If you want to invest in any short term market security in which security you will invest?and Why? consider you are the new investor

5. In market which will be easy for the investor

a) To keep physical form of security

b) Demat form

State along with the reason

Unit 2
Primary and Secondary Market

Define primary market

The primary market, also known as the new issue market, is a segment of the capital market where securities are issued to investors for the first time.

(The National Stock Exchange (NSE) and other stock exchanges are secondary markets)

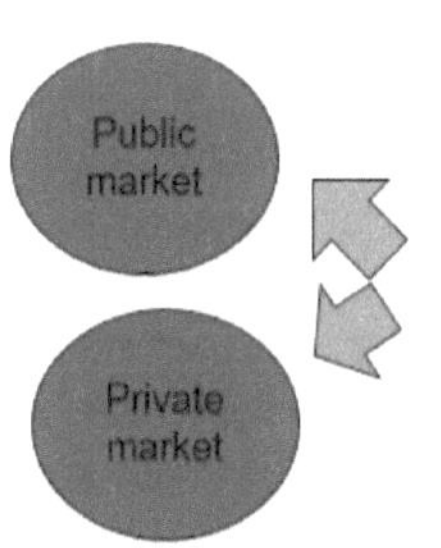

In the public market, securities are offered to the general public through an initial public offering (IPO).

Types of Primary Market

In the private market, securities are sold directly to institutional investors or high-net-worth individuals.

What is the role of primary market

a) The primary market provides the ***channel for sale of new securities.***

b) Primary market provides opportunity to issuers of securities; Government as well as corporates, to raise resources to meet their requirements of investment and/or discharge some obligation.

c) They may issue the securities at face value, or ***at a discount/premium and these securities may take a variety of forms such as equity, debt*** etc.

d) They may issue the securities ***in the domestic market and/or international market.***

What do you mean by face value of Shares

It is simply the price at which you purchase the shares of a particular company. Also known as the par value, face value is the value of the company as listed in its books and share certificates. It is fixed by the company, once it decides to issue its shares.

Shares can be issued at par or at discount or at premium.

Issued at par

For an equity share, the face value(at par) is usually a very small amount (Rs. 5, Rs. 10) and does not have much bearing on the price of the share, which may quote higher in the market, at Rs. 100 or Rs. 1,000 or any other price as the market decides.

Issued at premium

Issue of shares at the premium means the amount demanded by the company at the time of issue of shares is more than the face value of shares. It may serve as the security money or the goodwill money which is being demanded by the company.

Issued at Discount

The issue of shares at a discount means the issue of the shares at a price less than the face value of the share.Normally the shares are issued at par or at premium but not at discount.

Example

(Securities are generally issued in denominations of Rs. 5, Rs. 10 or Rs. 100. This is known as the Face Value or Par Value of the security as discussed earlier. When a security is sold above its face value, it is said to be issued at a Premium and if it is sold at less than its face value, then it is said to be issued at a Discount. Normally, issues are made at premium. Discount issues are rarely made.)

⟹ *Why do companies need to issue shares to public*

a) Most companies are usually started *privately by their promoter(s).* However, the promoters' capital and the borrowings from banks and financial institutions may not be sufficient for setting up or running the business over a long term, especially when the business grows and looks to expand. So companies invite the public to contribute towards the equity and issue shares to individual investors.

b) The way to invite share capital from the public is through a „Public Issue". Simply stated, a public issue is an offer to the public to subscribe to the share capital of a company. Once this is done, the company allots shares to the applicants as per the prescribed rules and regulations laid down by SEBI.

c) Companies may issue shares to raise capital and diversify ownership. This allows new investors to become shareholders and can bring new perspectives and ideas to the company.

a) **<u>Initial Public Offering (IPO)</u>:** IPO is when an unlisted company makes *<u>either a fresh issue of securities or an offer for sale of its existing securities or both for the first time to the public.</u>* This paves the way for listing and trading of the issuer's securities

b) **<u>A follow on public offering</u>:** (Further Issue) is when an already listed company makes either a fresh issue of securities to the public or an offer for sale to the public, *<u>through an offer document.</u>*

c) *<u>Rights Issue</u>: It is when a listed company proposes to issue fresh securities to its existing shareholders as on a record date. The rights are normally offered in a particular ratio to the number of securities held prior to the issue.* (For example, in a rights issue of 1:1, one new equity share is issued for every equity share held by the shareholders. Hence, the shareholding of the investor doubles after the rights issue. This route is best suited for companies who would like to raise capital without diluting the stake of its existing shareholders)

d) *<u>A Preferential issue</u>:* It is an issue of shares or of convertible securities by listed companies to a select group of persons under Section 62 of the Companies Act, 2013 which is neither a rights issue nor a public issue. This is a faster way for a company to raise equity capital. The issuer company has to comply with the Companies Act and the requirements contained in the Chapter pertaining to preferential allotment in SEBI guidelines which inter- alia include pricing, disclosures in notice etc.

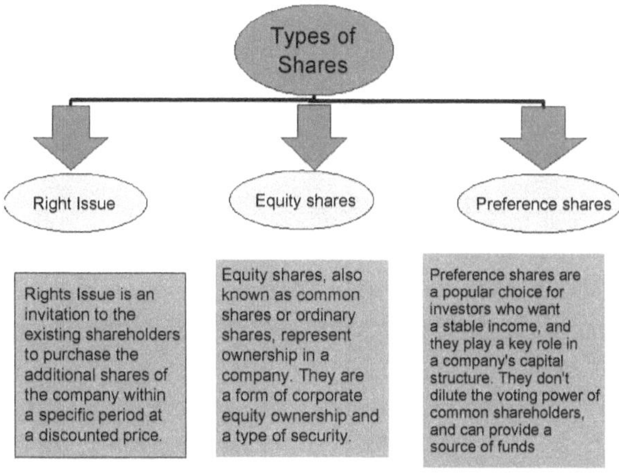

Issue price :- The price at which a company initially offers shares at the market is called the issue price. The market price might be below or higher than the issue price

Market capitalisation:- The market value of a quoted company, which is calculated by multiplying its current share price (market price) by the number of shares in issue, is called market capitalization. E.g. Company A has 120 million shares in issue. The current market price is Rs. 100. The market capitalisation of company A is Rs. 12000 million

What is the difference between public issue and private placement?

a) When an issue is not made to only a select set of people but is open to the general public and any other investor at large, it is a public issue. But if the issue is made to a select set of people, it is called private placement.

b) As per Companies Act, 2013, an issue becomes public if it results in allotment to 50 persons or more. This means an issue can be privately placed where an allotment is made to less than 50 persons excluding Qualified Institutional Buyers and Employee Stock Options.

WHAT IS AN INITIAL PUBLIC OFFER (IPO)?

a) An initial public offering (IPO) is when a private company sells shares of stock to the public for the first time.

b) It is when an unlisted company makes either a fresh issue of securities or an offer for sale of its existing securities or both for the first time to the public.

Both are done in primary market

Who decides the price of an issue?

a) The Indian primary market started in an era of free pricing in 1992. Following this, the guidelines have provided that the issuer in consultation with Merchant Banker shall decide the price.

b) There is *no price formula stipulated by SEBI.*

c) SEBI *does not play any role in price fixation.*

d) The company and merchant bankers are however required *to give full disclosures of the parameters which they had considered while deciding the issue price.*

e) There are two types of issues, *one where company and Lead Merchant Banker fix a price (called fixed price) and other, where the company and the Lead Manager (LM) stipulate a floor price or a price band and leave* _it to market forces to determine the final price_ (price discovery through book building process).

f) Nowadays, all issues are normally done through the book built route. However, the fixed price route has been kept open to allow small and medium enterprises to offer shares on the SME platform of the exchanges.

What does 'price discovery through Book Building Process' mean?

a) The book building process is a price discovery mechanism used by companies when issuing shares to the public for the first time.

b) It is a mechanism where, during the period for which the IPO is open, bids are collected from investors at various prices, which are above or equal to the floor price.

c) he offer price will be decided after the bid closing date

What is the main difference between offer of shares through book building and offer of shares through a normal public issue?

Prices at which securities are offered, are not known to the public through book building

But in case of normal public issue the prices are known to public in advance

But if the issue is made to a selected set of people, it is called private placement. As per Companies Act, 2013, an issue becomes public if it results in allotment to 50 persons or more. This means an issue can be privately placed where an allotment is made to less than 50 persons excluding Qualified Institutional Buyers and Employee Stock Options.

Distinguish between private and public limited company

Points	Private company	Public company
1) Meaning	A private company is a type of business entity that is privately owned, either by an individual or a group. Private companies can still issue company stock and raise capital from outside shareholders, but their shares do not trade on a public stock exchange.	A public company is a corporation wherein the ownership is dispensed to general public shareholders through the free trade of shares of stock over-the-counter at markets or on exchanges

2) Minimum members required	Minimum - 2 members Maximum - 50 members	Minimum - 7 members Maximum - No limit
3) Issue of securities	By way of right issue or bonus issue through private placement	To public through prospectus
4) Securities listed on stock exchange	Not applicable (However, with effect from 27 October 2023, the Ministry of Corporate Affairs, Government of India, has made it mandatory for private limited companies also to issue their securities in dematerialized form starting from 30 September 2024	Securities offered to public are listed in stock exchange

What is Cut-Off Price?

The cut-off price in an IPO is the price at which a company issues shares to investors. It is the minimum price that investors must bid to apply for the shares.

In a Book building issue, the issuer is required to indicate either the price band or a floor price in the prospectus. The actual discovered issue price can be any price in the price band or any price above the floor price.

Price band:- A price band is the range within which a stock's price can fluctuate. The stock exchange or seller sets the price band, which helps, manage mass stock trading and prevent market volatility.

This issue price is called —Cut-Off Price. The issuer and lead manager decides this after considering the book and the investors' appetite for the stock

What is minimum number of days for which a bid should remain open during book building?

The book should remain open for 3 days

Exception

(It's extendable by 3 days in case of a reworking in the price band. The issue can remain open for further than that period in case the company and the investment bankers consider it necessary. Most of the companies choose

3 days. Some of the factors in choosing bidding days on the smallest side are. In case companies need to extend the bidding, they can do it for 3 more days)

⟹ *Can open outcry system be used for book building?*

No. As per SEBI, only electronically linked transparent facilities are allowed to be used in case of book building.

⟹ *How does one know if shares are allotted in an IPO/offer for sale? What is the timeframe for getting refund if shares not allotted?*

a) As per SEBI (Issue of Capital and Disclosure Requirements) Regulations, 2009 the Basis of Allotment should be completed with 4 working days from the issue close date

b) As soon as the basis of allotment is completed, within a working day the details of credit to demat account / allotment advice and dispatch of refund order needs to be completed.

c) So an investor should *know in about 5 working days* time from the closure of issue, whether shares are allotted to him or not.

⟹ **What is ASBA?**

ASBA stands for Applications Supported by Blocked Amount. It is a process developed by India's Securities and Exchange Board (SEBI) for applying to Initial Public Offerings (IPOs).

a) In ASBA, an IPO applicant's account is not debited until shares are allotted to them. The process involves an investor *authorising a Self Certified Syndicate Bank (SCSB)* to block the application money in the bank account.

b) The funds can be blocked from the applicant's savings bank account or current account, *but not from overdraft or loan accounts*

c) If an investor is applying through ASBA, his application money shall be debited from the bank account only *if his/her application is selected for allotment after the basis of allotment is finalised*

d) Under ASBA, funds blocked in the account *will continue to earn interest during the application processing period, if held in an interest-bearing account.* Bank will mark a *lien on the deposit account of the investor to the extent of the application money.* The lien will be removed immediately after finalisation of the basis of allotment. If the bid is successful, the deposit account will be debited and the allotted shares will be transferred by the Company to the applicant's Demat account.

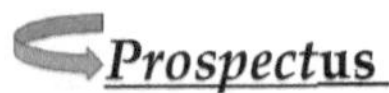

Role of Registrar

The registrar of an IPO issue is responsible for processing IPO applications, allocating the shares as per SEBI rules, processing refunds, and transferring allocated shares to investors' demat accounts. All registrars are registered with SEBI & Stock exchanges.

The Lead Manager coordinates with the Registrar to ensure follow up so that that the flow of applications from collecting bank branches, processing of the applications and other matters till the basis of allotment is finalised, dispatch security certificates and refund orders completed and securities listed

Prospectus

Meaning:

A prospectus is a legal document that provides information about an investment offering to the public. It is a formal document that is required by and filed with the Securities and Exchange Commission (SEC).

A large number of new companies float on public issues.

a) While a large number of these companies are genuine, a few may want to exploit the investors.Therefore, *it is very important that an investor before applying for any issue identifies the future potential of a company.*

b) A part of the guidelines issued by SEBI (Securities and Exchange Board of India) is the disclosure of information to the public. This *disclosure includes information like the reason for raising the money, the way money is proposed to be spent, the return expected on the money* etc.

c) This information is in the form of Prospectus' which also *includes information regarding the size of the issue, the current status of the company, its equity capital, its current and past performance, the promoters, the project, cost of the project, means of financing, product and capacity etc.* It also contains lot of mandatory information regarding underwriting and statutory compliances.

A prospectus can be defined as "prospectus, notice, circular, advertisement, letter, or communication, written or by radio or television, which offers any security for sale or confirms the sale of any security"

Types of
Prospectus

Red Herring Prospectus   Shelf Prospectus   Abridged Prospectus

1) Red Herring Prospectus:

It is the prospectus that *does not contain all the information regarding the prices of securities offered and the number of securities that are to be issued.* As per the provisions of the act, the firm must issue this prospectus to the registrar at least three times before the opening of the offer and the subscription list.

2) Shelf Prospectus:

It is stated under Section 31 of the Companies Act, 2013 and is issued *when a company or any public financial institution offers one or more securities to the public.* A company must provide *a period of validity of the prospectus, which shall not be more than one year.* An information *memorandum must be provided by the organisation when filing the Shelf Prospectus.*

3) Abridged Prospectus:

It is a kind of memorandum that contains *all the salient features of the prospectus as specified by SEBI (Securities and Exchange Board of India).* Abridged Prospectus includes all the information in brief, which provides a summary to the investor to make further decisions.

What does the draft offer document means

a) Draft Offer document' means the offer document in draft stage.

b) The draft offer documents are filed with SEBI, at least 30 days prior to the registration of red herring prospectus or prospectus with ROC.

c) SEBI may specify changes, if any, in the draft Offer Document and the issuer or the lead merchant banker shall carry out such changes in the draft offer document before filing the Offer Document with ROC.

d) The Draft Offer Document is available on the SEBI website for public comments for a period of 21 days from the filing of the Draft Offer Document with SEBI.

⟹ _Who prepares the prospectus?_

The merchant banker (lead manager) prepares and drafts the IPO prospectus with the help of the issuing company.

("Merchant Bankers are responsible for getting the project appraised, finalising the cost of the project, profitability estimates and for preparing of Prospectus")

⟹ _What is lock in period?_

Lock-in' indicates a _freeze on the sale of shares for a certain period of time._ SEBI guidelines have **stipulated lock-in requirements on shares of promoters mainly to ensure that the promoters or main persons, who are controlling the company,** shall continue to hold some minimum percentage in the company after the public issue

⟸ What is listing of securities

Listing securities is the process of allowing a company's securities to be traded on a recognized stock exchange.

Merits of Listing Security

- **Liquidity:** Listing securities provides liquidity.

- **Transparency:** Listing securities requires companies to disclose essential information, ensuring transparency.

- **Capital raising:** Listing securities enables a company to raise capital while strengthening its structure and reputation.

- **Increased exposure:** Listed companies receive greater exposure through IPOs, attracting investor interest and contributing to growth.

- Increased accountability: Listed securities increase accountability.

What is the listing agreement

a) At the time of listing securities of a company on a stock exchange, _the company is required to enter into a listing agreement with the exchange._

b) The listing agreement _specifies the terms and conditions of listing and the disclosures that shall be made by a company on a continuous basis to the exchange._

What does 'Delisting of securities' mean?

a) The term Delisting of securities' means permanent removal of securities of a listed company from a stock exchange.

b) As a consequence of delisting, the securities of that company would no longer be traded at that stock exchange.

WHAT IS SEBI'S ROLE IN AN ISSUE?

a) Any company _making a public issue or a listed company making a rights issue of value of more than Rs 50 lakhs_ is required to file a draft offer document with SEBI for its observations.

b) The company can _proceed further on the issue only after getting observations from SEBI._

c) The validity period of _SEBI's observation letter is three months only_ i.e. the company has to open its issue within three months period after the observations are issued by SEBI.

Does it mean that SEBI recommends an issue?

a) SEBI _does not recommend any issue nor does it take any responsibility either for the financial soundness of any scheme_ or the project for which the issue is proposed to be made or for the correctness of the statements made or opinions expressed in the offer document.

b) SEBI mainly _scrutinises the issue for seeing that adequate disclosures are made_ by the issuing company _in the prospectus or offer documents_

c) SEBI takes up _grievances related to issue and transfer of securities and non-payment of dividend_ with listed companies

d) In addition, _SEBI also takes up grievances against the various intermediaries registered with it and related issues._

Can companies in India raise foreign currency resources?

Yes. Indian companies are permitted to raise foreign currency resources through two main sources:

a) Issue of foreign currency convertible bonds more commonly known as FCCBs

b) Issue of ordinary shares through depository receipts namely **Global Depository Receipts (GDRs)/American Depository Receipts (ADRs)'** to foreign investors i.e. to the institutional investors or individual investors.

American Depositary Receipt

An American depositary receipt (ADR) *is a certificate that represents shares of a foreign company.* ADRs are *issued by US banks and traded on American stock exchanges.* ADRs are an easy way for US investors to own foreign stocks

1) *Sponsored ADR*

The foreign company that issues shares to the *public enters into an agreement with a US depositary bank to sell its shares in US markets.* The bank is responsible for record keeping, sale, and distribution of shares to the public, distribution of dividends, and more. The foreign company retains control over the ADR and usually pays the costs of issuance.

2) *Unsponsored ADR*

These shares trade *on the over-the-counter (OTC) market.* These shares are issued in accordance with market demand, and the foreign company has *no formal agreement with a depositary bank.* Unsponsored ADRs are often issued by more than one depositary bank.

(ADR are traded in the same manner as shares in U.S. companies, on the New York Stock Exchange (NYSE) and the American Stock Exchange (AMEX) or quoted on NASDAQ and the over the-counter (OTC) market)

What is meant by Global Depository Receipts?

A Global Depository Receipt (GDR) is a certificate issued by a depository bank that represents shares in a foreign company.

- GDRs are also known as international depository receipts (IDRs).

- GDRs are a type of financial instrument used to raise capital from international investors.

- They can be used by Indian companies to list their shares on foreign exchanges.

- GDRs are typically denominated in US dollars and traded on international stock exchanges.

- GDRs offer companies access to more capital and investors, the opportunity to invest in foreign companies' equity. They can also be a lower-cost way to invest in other countries.

Some disadvantages of GDRs include:

- Administrative fees

- Investors face economic risks due to the possibility of a recession, bank failures, or political unrest in the nation where the overseas company is based

- Dividends are paid in domestic countries' currency which is subject to volatility in the forex market

- It is mostly beneficial to High Net Worth Individual (HNI) investors due to their capacity to invest a high amount in GDR

Difference between ADR and GDR

ADRs are shares of a single foreign company issued in the U.S. GDRs are shares of a single foreign company issued in more than one country as part of a GDR program

- **Issuance Market:** ADRs are mainly issued in the US markets, while GDRs are issued globally in markets other than the US.

- **Trading Currency:** ADRs are traded in US dollars, whereas GDRs can be traded in any foreign currency.

- **Investors:** ADRs primarily attract US investors, whereas GDRs cater to investors worldwide.

- **Listing:** While ADRs can be listed on any US stock exchange, GDRs are typically listed on European stock exchanges.

- **Regulation:** ADRs are subject to regulations imposed by the US Securities and Exchange Commission. GDRs are regulated by the securities market regulator of the issuing country.

- **Sponsorship:** ADRs require sponsorship from a USbased bank, while GDRs need a sponsoring bank based in the country of listing.

- **Dividends:** Dividends on ADRs are paid in US dollars, while GDRs pay dividends in the currency of the country where they are issued.

- **Purpose:** ADRs are typically used by foreign companies to raise capital in the US, while GDRs are employed by companies to raise capital globally.

- **Issuing Company's Country of Origin:** Companies issuing ADRs are typically based outside the US. In contrast, companies issuing GDRs can be based anywhere, including the US.

- **Taxation:** Taxation on ADRs and GDRs differ according to the regulations of the respective issuing country.

What is meant by Foreign Currency Convertible Bonds?

Meaning

As per definition given by RBI, Foreign Currency Convertible Bond' (FCCB) means a bond issued by an Indian company expressed in foreign currency, and the principal and interest in respect of which is payable in foreign currency'.

Foreign currency convertible bonds (FCCBs) are financial instruments that are issued in a currency other than the issuer's home currency. FCCBs are a type of bond that acts as both a debt and equity instrument.

FCCBs have the following features:

- *Convertible:* FCCBs can be converted into a predetermined number of shares of the issuer's stock at a later date.

- *Debt and equity:* FCCBs act like a bond, making regular coupon and principal payments. They also allow investors to convert them into equity.

- *Maturity:* The maturity of an FCCB must not be less than 5 years.

- *Conversion rate:* Upon maturity, the holders can convert the equivalent value of equity at a set conversion rate.

- *Option to retain bonds:* FCCB holders can also retain the bonds.

What is meant by the Secondary market?

A secondary market is a marketplace *where investors buy and sell securities that were previously issued.*

In the secondary market, securities are traded after they are initially offered in the primary market.

The secondary market provides investors with liquidity, enabling them to sell their securities easily and quickly if they need to raise cash

What is the role of Secondary Market

The Securities and Exchange Board of India (SEBI) is the primary regulatory authority for securities markets in India. SEBI's secondary market department has several roles, including:

a) Monitoring and control

Secondary equity markets monitor and control companies by:

- Promoting value-enhancing control activities
- Enabling implementation of incentive-based management contracts
- Aggregating information (via price discovery) that guides management decisions

b) Price discovery

The secondary market facilitates price discovery by allowing investors to trade securities based on the supply and demand dynamics of the market

c) Liquidity

The secondary market provides liquidity and marketability to existing securities

d) Trade exit or entry

Investors can exit or enter any listed security via secondary markets

Difference between Primary market and Secondary Market

Points	Primary market	Secondary Market
1) *Role*	A capital Market where security are issued first time	A capital Market for trading previously issued securities
2) *Alternative name*	New issue market	After issue Market
3) *Products*	Corporate or government bonds, fresh stock of companies, notes, and bills	Equity shares, preference shares, bonds, debentures
4) *Intermediaries*	Investment banks and other underwriter firms	Brokers
5) *Type of purchasing*	Direct	Indirect

6) *Parties involved*	Buying and selling takes place between the issuing company and investors	Buying and selling takes place among investors and traders without the involvement of the issuing company
7) *Price of the shares*	Remains fixed	Fluctuates depending on changes in supply and demand
8) *Beneficiary*	Issuing company	Investors

Role of stock exchange in buying and selling of shares

a) A stock exchange brings companies and investors together. A stock exchange helps companies raise capital or money by issuing equity shares to be sold to investors. The companies invest those funds back into their business, and investors, ideally, profit from their investment in those companies.

b) Stock exchange is the trading platform provided by NSE, an electronic one and there is no need for buyers and sellers to meet at a physical location to trade. They can trade through the computerised trading screens available with the NSE trading members or the internet based trading facility provided by the trading members of NSE

Demutualisation

Demutualisation refers to legal structure where there is segregation of ownership, management and trading rights

Mutual Exchange

a) In a mutual exchange, the three functions of ownership, management and trading are concentrated into a single Group.

b) Here, the broker members of the exchange are both the owners and the traders on the exchange and they further manage the exchange as well. This at times can lead to conflicts of interest in decision making

How is depositary is similar to bank

In financial terms, a depository means an entity that holds financial securities in a dematerialized form.

Earlier, securities were issued and transacted in physical form. For transferring securities, depositories maintained manual records on a leaf of paper

1.   *A bank holds cash on behalf of its customers, while a depository holds securities like bonds, shares, and mutual fund units.*

2.   *Bank Transfer funds between accounts on the instruction of the account holder Depositary transfer securities between accounts on the instruction of the account holder.*

3.   *Bank Facilitates transfers without having to handle money. Depositary facilitates transfers of ownership without having to handle securities*

Which are depositories in India

1.   The National Securities Depository Limited (NSDL)

2.   Central Depository Services (India) Limited (CDSL).

What are the benefits of participation in a depositary

*   Immediate transfer of securities

*   No stamp duty on transfer of securities

*   Elimination of risks associated with physical certificates such as bad delivery, fake securities, etc.

*   Reduction in paperwork involved in transfer of securities

*   Reduction in transaction cost

*   Ease of nomination facility

*   Change in address recorded with DP gets registered electronically with all companies in which investor holds securities eliminating the need to correspond with each of them separately

*   Transmission of securities is done directly by the DP eliminating correspondence with companies

*   Convenient method of consolidation of folios/accounts

*   Holding investments in equity, debt instruments and Government securities in a single account; automatic credit into demat account, of shares, arising out of split/consolidation/merger etc.

Depository Participant

A depository participant (DP) is a registered *stockbroker or intermediary between investors and depositories in India.* DPs act as a **link between investors**

and depositories, maintain investor-level accounts for securities, and facilitate the trading process.

A DP can be a stockbroker, bank, or financial institution that helps act as a medium between a trader or investor and the stock exchange.

Important Note:-

1. *The depository has not prescribed any minimum balance. You can have zero balance in your account.*

2. *ISIN (International Securities Identification Number) is a unique identification number for a security.*

Custodian

a) A custodian is a clearing member of the National Stock Exchange of India (NSE). Custodians are not trading members, but they settle trades on behalf of their clients.

b) Custodians help investors by keeping track of and ensuring the safety of their investments. They help minimise the potential risk of mishandling physical securities and investor records.

c) Custodians typically offer trade settlements, foreign exchange transactions, and tax services.

Important points:-

- *In order to dematerialise physical securities one has to fill in a Demat Request Form (DRF) which is available with the DP and submit the same along with physical certificates one wishes to dematerialise. Separate DRF has to be filled for each ISIN number*

- *Odd lot share certificates can also be dematerialised.*

- *If one wishes to get back your securities in the physical form one has to fill in the Remat Request Form (RRF) and request your DP for rematerialisation of the balances in your securities account. This process is called dematerialisation*

- *Dematerialised shares do not have any distinctive numbers. These shares are fungible, which means that all the holdings of a particular security will be identical and interchangeable.*

The trading on stock exchanges in India _used to take place through open outcry_ without use of information technology for immediate matching or recording of trades. This was time consuming and inefficient. This _imposed limits on trading volumes and efficiency_. In order to provide efficiency, liquidity and transparency, NSE introduced a nationwide, on-line, fully-automated screen based trading system (SBTS)

A screen-based trading system (SBTS) _is a computerised platform that allows users to buy and sell securities._ In India, the _National Stock Exchange (NSE) and the Bombay Stock Exchange (BSE) are the primary stock exchanges._ Both exchanges have their own trading software, **NEAT for NSE and BOLT for BSE**.

SBTS allows members to enter the quantities of shares and prices they want to transact at on a computer. The transaction will be executed as soon as a quote that matches the member's entry or buys a quote from a counterparty.

Features of screen based trading

SBTS has several features that distinguish it from traditional floor-trading systems:

a) _Direct market participants_

SBTS can link directly with market participants at remote locations without the need to route orders through intermediaries on an exchange floor.

b) _Full anonymity_

SBTS provides full anonymity by accepting orders from members without revealing their identity.

c) _Efficiency, liquidity, and transparency_

SBTS is a fully-automated system that provides efficiency, liquidity, and transparency

⟹ *What is NEAT*

a) NSE is the first exchange in the world to use satellite communication technology for trading. Its trading system, called National Exchange for Automated Trading (NEAT), is a state-of-the-art client server based application.

b) At the server end all trading information is stored in an in-memory database to achieve minimum response time and maximum system availability for users.

c) It has an uptime record of 99.7%. For all trades entered into NEAT system, there is uniform response time of less than one second

➤ _Contract Notes_

A Contract Note is a document provided by the stock broker to its customer on the day when the customer traded with them. This document captures all the transactions or trades on a particular day, brokerage fee and taxes. It is a reference point for clients to see their trades and the corresponding prices.

It is the _legal obligation of the stock broker_ to send a contract note to the customer who traded on a particular day. A contract note sent via E-mail is called an 'Electronic Contract Note' (ECN) or a 'Digital Contract Note'.

Features:-

a) It also helps to _settle disputes/claims between the investor and the trading member._

b) It is a _prerequisite for filing a complaint or arbitration_ proceeding against the trading member in case of a dispute.

c) A valid contract note _should be in the prescribed form, contain the details of trades, stamped with requisite value and duly signed by the authorised signatory._

d) Contract notes are _kept in duplicate,_ the trading member and the client should keep one copy each.

e) After verifying the details contained therein, the client keeps one copy and returns the second copy to the trading member duly acknowledged by him

Note:

- The Contract Note is printed on legal stamp paper (e-Stamp).

- The PDF of the Contract Note is sent via email to the customer at end of the day.

- It can also be downloaded from the broker's back-office website or mobile app.

- It is sent only to customers who traded on a particular day.

- Only a stock broker can issue a Contract Note for trades done through them. Contract notes must be issued within 24 hours of the execution of trades.

- Old Contract Notes can be downloaded from broker's the back office website or app

Details of contract note:-

- Name, address, and SEBI Registration number of the stock broker.

- Name of the partners, proprietor, and the Authorised Signatory for the stock broker.

- The dealing office details and PAN details of the stock broker.

- The Unique Client Code and PAN of the Investor.

- The Contract note number, date of issue of the contract note, the settlement number (a 7 digit number that is a combination of the first 4 digits representing year and last 4 digits representing a running serial number), and the period for settlement.

- The order number and order time corresponding to the trades.

- The trade number and trade time.

- The quantity and details of securities bought/sold by the client.

- The trade price and the brokerage (mentioned separately).

- Service tax rates and any other charges levied by the broker.

- Securities Transaction Tax (STT) as applicable.

- Signature of the Authorised Signatoryfor the stock broker

What is the maximum brokerage that a broker can charge?

The maximum brokerage that can be charged by a broker from his clients as commission ***cannot be more than 2.5%*** of the value mentioned in the respective purchase or sale note. However, *it is upto the broker to charge less and many also do so.* Hence, ***SEBI only prescribes the maximum brokerage chargeable and not the minimum.***

WHAT PRECAUTIONS MUST ONE TAKE BEFORE INVESTING IN THE STOCK MARKETS?

- *Registered broker:-*

Make sure your broker is registered with SEBI and the exchanges and do not deal with unregistered intermediaries.

- *Contract note:-*

Ensure that you receive contract notes for all your transactions from your broker within one working day of execution of the trades.

- ***Risk taking and tolerance:-***

All investments carry risk of some kind. Investors should always know the risk that they are taking and invest in a manner that matches their risk tolerance.

- ***Rumours:-***

Do not be misled by market rumours, wrong advertisement or _hot tips' of the day.

- ***Firm decision:-***

Take informed decisions by studying the fundamentals of the company.

- ***Market analysis***

Find out the business the company is into, its future prospects, quality of management, past track record etc. Sources of knowing about a company are through annual reports, economic magazines, databases available with vendors or your financial advisor.

- ***Be careful:-***

If your financial advisor or broker advises you to invest in a company you have never heard of, be cautious. Spend some time checking out about the company before investing.

- ***If you want then only invest:-***

Do NOT invest in any security or company that you are not comfortable with even if the broker strongly recommends. You should be firm and invest only where you want to.

- ***Own Analysis:-***

Do not be attracted by announcements of fantastic results/news reports, about a company. Do your own research before investing in any stock.

- ***Be aware of fraud:-***

Do not be attracted to stocks based on what an internet website promotes, unless you have done adequate study of the company.

- ***No guaranteed return:-***

a) Investing in very low priced stocks or what are known as penny stocks does not guarantee high returns.

b) Be cautious about stocks which show a sudden spurt in price or trading activity.

c) Any advice or tip that claims that there are huge returns expected, especially for acting quickly, may be risky and may lead to losing some, most, or all of your money.

WHAT RESOURCES ARE AVAILABLE TO INVESTOR/CLIENT FOR REDRESSING HIS GRIEVANCES?

a) *Arbitration*

Arbitration is an **alternative dispute resolution mechanism provided by the Exchange for resolving disputes between the trading members** and between trading members & constituents (i.e. clients of trading members), in respect of trades done on the Exchange. **This process of resolving a dispute is comparatively faster than other means of redressal.**

* *Who can work under Arbitration*

The Exchange provides a list of **eligible persons approved by SEBI for each of the Regional Arbitration centres.** Persons who form part of the list of Arbitrators are the ones **who possess an expertise in their respective fields including banking, finance, legal (judges) and capital market areas**

* *Who can avail the facility of arbitration*

- Investors who have dealt on the Exchange through its trading members and who possess a valid contract note issued by the trading member of the Exchange.

- Investors who have dealt on the Exchange through registered sub-brokers of the trading members of NSE and who possess valid sale/purchase note issued by the registered sub-broker.

- Trading members who have a claim, dispute or difference with another trading member or a constituent.

b) *Investor protection fund*

NSE has established an Investor Protection Fund *with the objective of compensating investors in the event of defaulters'* assets not being sufficient to meet the admitted claims of investors, promoting investor education, awareness and research

Payments out of the IPF may include claims *arising of non payment/ non receipt of securities by the investor from the trading member who has been declared a defaulter.* The maximum amount of claim payable from the IPF to the investor (where the trading member through whom the investor has dealt is declared a defaulter) is Rs. 15 lakh.

SEBI SCORES or SEBI REDRESSAL SYSTEM

There will be occasions when you have a **complaint against a listed company/ intermediary** registered with SEBI. In the event of such a complaint you should first approach the concerned company/ intermediary against whom you have a complaint. However, you may not be satisfied with their response. Therefore, you should know whom you should turn to, to get your complaint redressed.

SEBI takes up complaints related to issue and transfer of securities and non-payment of dividend with listed companies. In addition, SEBI also takes up complaints against the various intermediaries registered with it and related issues

a) SCORES is a web based centralised grievance redress system of SEBI

b) SCORES enables investors to lodge and follow up their complaints and track the status of redressal of such complaints online from the above website from anywhere. This enables the market intermediaries and listed companies to receive the complaints online from investors, redress such complaints and report redressal online.

c) All the activities starting from lodging of a complaint till its closure by SEBI would be online in an automated environment and the complainant can view the status of his complaint online.

d) An investor, who is not familiar with SCORES or does not have access to SCORES, can lodge complaints in physical form at any of the offices of SEBI. Such complaints would be scanned and also uploaded in SCORES for processing.

PRODUCTS IN THE SECONDARY MARKETS

What are the products dealt in the Secondary Markets?

1) Equity shares :-

Equity shares are representative of stakes in ownership of a company. If, for instance, Ms.Priya holds Rs. 10,000 worth of equity shares in Company M, then she holds a stake equivalent to that amount in that organisation.

Apart from equity shares, companies can also issue preference shares. However, a company's primary source of raising capital is via the different types of equity shares. Usually, companies confer an array of entitlements to holders of equity shares.

Benefits enjoyed by equity shareholders:

a) One of the primary entitlements that equity shareholders enjoy is voting rights.

b) They can exercise such voting rights in regard to a company's policies as well as the election of directors.

c) However, based on different types of equity shares, the weight of each share in relation to voting count may vary. But, typically, a single stock is equivalent to one vote.

d) Alongside voting rights, equity shareholders are also entitled to attend general meetings and annual general meetings of an organisation.

e) Plus, they enjoy dividend payments; although, companies are not bound to disburse dividends periodically to equity shareholders, and the payment does not follow any fixed rate.

**(Equity shares are having a right to get bonus and right shares whenever declared by the company)**

a) _Bonus shares_

As the name might suggest, bonus shares are those stocks that companies issue to the existing shareholders without any additional charge. Through the issuance of bonus shares, companies can convert their retained earnings into stocks.

**Usually, companies provide these bonus shares to shareholders instead of paying out dividends.**

Furthermore, organisations issue bonus shares _**on a pro-rata basis.**_

For Example:-, if Mr. Amit holds 200 shares of Hindustan Unilever Ltd and the company announces its decision to issue 1:4 as a bonus, then he will receive 50 additional shares for free.

b) _Right shares_

Right shares refer to the offerings that a company makes to its existing shareholders to purchase new shares at a specific price within a particular period.

- In other words, the right shares are those new stocks on which existing stakeholders can lay claim before such issuing companies open them up to public trading.

- Similar to bonus shares, companies issue the right shares on a pro-rata basis as well. Therefore, if a company is offering 2000 new shares, and a shareholder possesses 2% of its existing lot, then he/she is entitled to 40 of those new offerings.

2) Preference shareholders:-

Preference shareholders are preferred stocks that come with a preferential right when it comes to _**a) the distribution of dividends or b) during the liquidation of a company.**_

It means, in both situations, preference shareholders are given more priority than other shareholders.

a) Typically, preference shares are released to raise capital for the company, which in turn is known as preference share capital.

b) It must be noted that preferred stockholders are partial owners of a company, but unlike common shares, preferred shares do not come with any voting rights.

However, shareholders' opinions may be taken into consideration during dissolution or altering the functions of an existing venture. Notably, the decision to announce dividends on preference shares lies entirely on the company's management.

a) *Cumulative Preference Shares*

These shares come with a provision that entitles shareholders to receive dividends in arrears. So, when a company does not make enough profits in a year to pay dividends, they pay cumulative dividends in the following year.

For Example:-Suppose a company Star Labs Private Limited *issues cumulative preference shares for Rs. 1000 each and promises to pay 10% as dividend annually.* Ideally, in a good economy, shareholders would *earn Rs. 100 on their investment.* However, owing to low returns, the company *could only pay Rs. 50 as a dividend that year*.

Subsequently, in the next year with the worsening condition, the company could not pay the dividend of Rs. 100. Once profits were generated, the company decided to pay off the current dividend along with the outstanding dividend of Rs. 150 to shareholders. So cumulatively, the company paid Rs. 250 as dividend to shareholders.

b) *Cumulative Convertible Preference Shares*

A type of preference shares where the dividend payable on the same accumulates, if not paid. Convertible shares are fundamentally those shares which enable holders to get them converted into equity shares at a fixed rate. Notably, these shares can only be converted after the expiry of a specified time and within a given period, as stated in the memorandum.

Ideally, these shares are considered to be beneficial for those investors who intend to receive preferred share dividends

3) Bonds

Bonds are an investment product where you lend your money to a government, municipality, or corporation at an agreed interest rate for a certain amount of time. In return, the issuer agrees to pay you interest and in most cases, to return the principal when the bond matures.

Features Of bonds

I.   **Interest Rate:** The interest rate is the coupon the bond issuer pays to the bondholder. Typically, it is a fixed percentage of the face value of the bond and is paid out periodically over the bond's life.

II. **Maturity date:** The maturity date refers to the redemption date, and the bond issuer must repay the bond's principal amount to the bondholder. It is the date on which the bond "matures."

III. **Face value:** The face value is the amount the bond issuer will pay the bondholder at maturity. It is also known as the par value of the bond.

IV. **Yield:** The yield is the rate of return on a bond. It is a percentage of the bond's current market price. It considers both the coupon rate and the bond's current market price.

V.   **Credit rating:** Credit rating agencies assign a bond rating based on the issuer's creditworthiness. This rating reflects the likelihood that the issuer will default on its bond payments.

VI. **Liquidity:** Bonds can be bought and sold in the secondary market so that investors can sell their bonds before maturity. The liquidity of a bond refers to the ease with which it can be bought or sold in the secondary market

Types of Bonds

1) Zero coupon bonds

Zero-coupon bonds are issued at a discount to their face value and do not pay periodic interest. Instead, they offer a fixed return at maturity, i.e., the difference between the issue price and face value. They are ideal for investors who want to lock in a fixed return for a specific period.

2) Treasury Bonds

The central government issues treasury bonds. Hence, it is the safest type of bond because there is no credit risk. These bonds have a maturity period of ten to thirty years and pay a fixed interest rate, which is a factor in the prevailing market conditions.

3) *Convertible Bonds*

The issuing company can convert these bonds into equity shares of the issuing company's stock at a pre-determined conversion ratio.

Equity investment

Why should one invest in equity

When you buy a share of a company you become a shareholder in that company. Shares are also known as Equities. Equities have the potential to increase in value over time. Research studies have proved that the equity returns have outperformed the returns of most other forms of investments in the long term.

a) Equities are considered the most rewarding, when compared to other investment options if held over a long duration.

b) Equity funds invest in stocks that are traded on the market. The sale and purchase of stocks make the funds highly liquid. Similarly, investors can easily redeem the equity fund units whenever they wish to. Once they redeem it, the money equal to the value of the units at the time of sale will be deposited in your account within a few days.

c) However, this does not mean all equity investments would guarantee similar high returns. Equities are high risk investments. Though higher the risk, higher the potential returns, high risk also indicates that the investor stands to lose some or all his investment amount if prices move unfavourably. One needs to study equity markets and stocks in which investments are being made carefully, before investing.

Which are the factors that influence the price of a stock?

Broadly there are two factors:

1) *Stock specific:-*

The stock-specific factor is related to people's expectations about the company, its future earnings capacity, financial health and management, level of technology and marketing skills. These factors depend on the performance of any particular company.

2) *Market specific:-*

The market specific factor is influenced by the investor's sentiment towards the stock market as a whole. On the other hand, unfavourable events like war, economic crisis, communal riots, minority government etc. depress the market irrespective of certain companies performing well.

However, the effect of market-specific factors is generally short-term. Despite ups and downs, the price of a stock in the long run stabilises based on the stock-specific factors. Therefore, a prudent advice to all investors is to analyse and invest and not speculate in shares.

What is meant by the terms Growth Stock / Value Stock?

Growth Stock:-

Growth stocks are stocks of companies whose revenue is growing faster than average. Growth stocks typically don't pay dividends, reinvesting profits into their growth instead. Investors buy growth stocks with the hope that share prices will rise quickly.

Value Stock:-

- The task here is to look for stocks that have been overlooked by other investors and which may have a hidden value'.

- These companies may have been beaten down in price because of some bad event, or may be in an industry that's not fancied by most investors.

- However, even a company that has seen its stock price decline still has assets to its name - buildings, real estate, inventories, subsidiaries, and so on.

- Many of these assets still have value, yet that value may not be reflected in the stock's price. Value investors look to buy stocks that are undervalued, and then hold those stocks until the rest of the market realises the real value of the company's assets.

- Value investors tend to purchase a company's stock usually based on relationships between the current market price of the company and certain business fundamentals.

What do you mean by portfolio

A portfolio is a collection of financial assets, such as stocks, bonds, commodities, cash, and real estate. It can be held by an individual, corporation, or financial institution

What do you mean by Diversification

Investing in many different securities and types of assets so that your overall return doesn't depend too much on any single investment

What are the benefits of Diversified portfolio

1) _Reduced risk_

A diversified portfolio can help reduce the overall risk of your portfolio. This is because your investments are spread across different asset classes, industries, and sectors.

2) _Higher returns_

In the long run, a diversified portfolio can generate higher risk-adjusted returns than a non-diversified portfolio.

3) _Reduced impact of market volatility_

A diversified portfolio can help reduce the overall risk associated with the portfolio.

4) _Protection from extreme market movement_

A diversified portfolio can help protect you from extreme movement in the market due to any single investment.

It is really just the simple practice of not putting all your eggs in one basket.‖ If you spread your investments across various types of assets and markets, you'll reduce the risk of your entire portfolio getting affected by the adverse returns of any single asset class

Debt instrument

Debt instruments are debt securities that can be bought and sold between two parties.

In Indian securities markets, the term „bond" is used for debt instruments issued by the Central and State governments and public sector organisations and the term „debenture" is used for instruments issued by private corporate sector

Features of Debt instrument

- _Maturity date:_ The date on which the borrower has agreed to repay the principal

- _Coupon rate:_ The interest rate

- _Return on capital:_ The amount borrowed

- _Issue date and issue price:_ The date and price at which the debt instrument is issued

- _Interest rate:_ The fixed interest rate for the period the investor holds the bond

- _Term-to-maturity,_ which is the number of years remaining for the bond to mature

- _Charge over the assets,_ which means the company may need to pledge or mortgage their assets to keep their funds safe for redemption

What are the segments in debt market

It consists of two main categories - the government securities market (G-Sec) and the corporate bond market. The government securities market encompasses securities issued by the central and state governments to fund the fiscal deficit. Sovereign securities are issued by the RBI on behalf of the Government of India.

Ex-date

An ex-date is the day when a stock starts trading without the value of its next dividend payment. It is typically one business day before the record date

Ex-dividend date

The ex-dividend date for stocks is usually set one business day before the record date. If you purchase a stock on its ex-dividend date or after, you will not receive the next dividend payment. Instead, the seller gets the dividend. If you purchase before the ex-dividend date, you get the dividend.

No-delivery period

In the Indian stock market, the no-delivery period refers to a period of time during which the delivery of shares is not allowed for settlement of trades. During this period, traders and investors can only buy or sell shares for intraday trading or for trading in the derivatives segment.

Book-Closure and record date

a) Book closure and record date

It helps a company _determine exactly the shareholders of company as on a given date._ Book closure refers to the closing of the register of the names of investors in the records of a company.

b) Companies announce book closure dates from time to time. The benefits of dividends, bonus issues, rights issue accrue to investors _whose name appears on the company's records as on a given date_ which is known as the record date and is declared in advance by the company so that buyers have enough time to buy the shares, get them registered in the books of the company and become entitled for the benefits such as bonus, rights, dividends etc.

c) With the depositories now in place, the buyers need not send shares physically to the companies for registration. This is taken care by the depository since they have the records of investor holdings as on a particular date electronically with them

Pay in and pay out day

Pay in day is the day when the brokers shall make payment or delivery of securities to the exchange. Pay out day is the day when the exchange makes payment or delivery of securities to the broker

What is Auction

On account of non-delivery of securities by the trading member on the pay-in day, the securities are put up for auction by the Exchange. This ensures that the buying trading member receives the securities. The Exchange purchases the requisite quantity in auction market and gives them to the buying trading member

What is the bad delivery

A tender of securities on a stock exchange that are not in proper transferable or negotiable form or not in compliance with the terms of a contract or the rules of an exchange.

Securities given for delivery *could be mutilated or damaged or without signature or proper form.* These would then be returned to the seller for appropriate action. Now the issue is relatively unimportant on account of electronic trades.

What is the clearing corporation

A clearing corporation is an organisation that is affiliated with a stock exchange. Its primary function is to oversee the handling of transactions, including confirmation, settlement, and delivery. Clearing corporations are also known as clearing firms or clearing houses

What is the rolling settlement

Rolling settlement is a process in India where trades are settled on T+2 days, which means that it takes two additional trading days after the trading date to complete the settlement.

The Rolling settlement system was introduced in India on Jan. 10, 2000 when 10 scrip's were put in the compulsory rolling settlement. Initially, the settlement period was T+5 but it has been gradually reduced toT+2 with effect from April 1, 2003. Since 2000, all other shares have been brought gradually in the compulsory rolling settlement system. It may be noted that there are some shares put in the T-Category.

In NSE, the trades pertaining to the rolling settlement are settled on a T+2 day basis where T stands for the trade day. Hence trades executed on a Monday are typically settled on the following Wednesday (considering 2 working days from the trade day). The funds and securities pay-in and pay-out are carried out on T+2 day. An investor has to deliver the securities to the trading member immediately upon getting the contract note for sale but in any case, before the prescribed securities pay-in day. In case of buying, he has to pay the amount to the trading member in such a manner that the amount paid is realised before the funds pay-in day.

Corporate Action

- Corporate actions are actions taken by a company that impact the shareholders value directly. It is an event that brings material changes to a company and affects its stakeholders.

- These may be either monetary e.g. dividend, or non-monetary e.g. Bonus, rights, or stock splits.

The different types of corporate actions announced by a company are:

- Rights issue

- Dividend

- Stock Split

- Conversion of debentures into shares

- Amalgamation

- Merger

- Demerger

- Capital reduction / Consolidation of shares

- Buy Back

- Bonus

- Open Offer

When a company announces a corporate action, it is initiating a process that will bring actual change to its securities either in terms of number of shares increasing in the hands on the shareholders or a change to the face value of the security or receiving shares of a new company by the shareholders as in the case of merger or acquisition etc.

By understanding these different types of processes and their effects, an investor can have a clearer picture of what a corporate action indicates about a company's financial affairs and how that action will influence the company's share price and performance.

➡️ _What is meant by 'Dividend' declared by companies?_

Returns received by investors in equities come in two forms

a) Growth in the value (market price) of the share and

b) Dividends.

Dividend is the _**distribution of part of a company's earnings to shareholders,**_ usually twice a year in the form of a final dividend and an interim dividend.

Dividend is therefore _a source of income for the shareholder._

- A dividend declaration is a statement made by the board of directors about dividend distribution.

- The declaration usually includes a record date, which is the date on which shareholders must be on record **(their name should appear in the registrar of company)** to receive the dividend payment.

- Normally, the dividend is expressed on a per share' basis, for instance - Rs. 3 per share. This makes it easy to see how much of the company's profits are being paid out, and how much are being retained by the company to plough back into the business.

(Until paid, dividends declared are a liability of the corporation)

➡️ _Dividend Yield_

Dividend yield gives the relationship between the current price of a stock and the dividend paid by its issuing company during the last 12 months.

Dividend Yield = Annual Dividend earned /Market price of the share *100

It is calculated by aggregating past year's dividend and dividing it by the current stock price.

Example: ABC Co. Share price: Rs. 360 Annual dividend: Rs. 10

Dividend Yield = Annual Dividend earned /Market price of the share *100

Dividend Yield = (10/360)x 100

Dividend yield: 2.77%

Important points

1. Historically, a higher dividend yield has been considered to be desirable among investors.

2. A high dividend yield is considered to be evidence that a stock is underpriced, whereas a low dividend yield is considered evidence that the stock is overpriced.

3. There have been companies in the past which had a record of high dividend yield, only to go bust in later years.

4. Dividend yield therefore can be only one of the factors in determining future performance of a company.

Stock Split

A stock split happens when a company *increases the number of its shares to boost the stock's liquidity.*

Although the number of shares outstanding increases by a specific multiple, the total *market value of all shares outstanding remains the same* because a split does not fundamentally change the company's value.

*   A stock split is done, when a company increases the number of its outstanding shares **to boost the stock's liquidity**.

*   Although the number of shares outstanding increases, there is **no change to the company's total market capitalization as the price of each share will split as well.**

*   A company elects to perform a stock split **to intentionally lower the price of a single share, making the company's stock more affordable without losing value.**

(*For Example:* If a company has issued 1,00,00,000 shares with a face value of Rs. 10 and the current market price being Rs. 100, a 2-for-1 stock split would reduce the face value of the shares to 5 and increase the number of the company's outstanding shares to 2,00,00,000, (1,00,00,000*(10/5)).

Consequently, the share price would also have to Rs. 50 so that the market capitalization or the value shares held by an investor remains unchanged. It is the same thing as exchanging a Rs. 100 note for two Rs. 50 notes; the value remains the same.)

Buy back of shares

A share buyback is also known as a stock buyback or share repurchase. In simple terms, the share buyback meaning is a financial strategy adopted by companies to repurchase their outstanding shares from the market or existing shareholders. As unlikely as it may sound, this share buyback holds its own importance.

Reasons of buy back is that Company wants to improve the liquidity of their shares and enhance shareholders health

Under the SEBI (Buy Back of Securities) Regulation, 1998,

A company is permitted to buy back its share from:

- Existing shareholders on a proportionate basis through the offer document.

- Open market through stock exchanges using a book building process.

- Shareholders holding odd lot shares.

Choose the correct option

1) __________ provides the channel for sale of new securities.

   a) **Primary market**

   b) Secondary market

   c) National stock exchange

   d) SEBI

2) Primary market provides opportunity to ________ their requirements of investment and/or discharge some obligation.

   a) Issuers of the securities

   b) Government

   c) Corporate

   d) **All of the above**

3) ___________ is the original cost of the stock shown on the certificate; for bonds, it is the amount paid to the holder at maturity.

   a) Face value of the security

   b) Par value of the security

   c) Security issued at premium

   d) **Either a or b**

4)   The price at which the security trades depends on the _________ in the economy.

a) Demand of the economy

b) Supply of the economy

c) **Fluctuation in the interest rate**

d) Political policies of the economy

5)   Normally, issues are made at

a) Face value

b) **Premium**

c) Discount

d) Depends upon the market

6)   Most companies are usually started privately by their _________

a) Board of directors

b) CEO

c) **Promoters**

d) None of the above

7)   _________ is when an unlisted company makes either a fresh issue of securities or an offer for sale of its existing securities or both for the first time to the public.

a) **Initial Public Offering (IPO)**

b) A follow on public offering

c) Rights Issue

d) A Preferential issue

8)   The price at which a company's shares are offered initially in the primary market is called as _______

a) Market price

b) Base price

c) **Issue price**

d) Selling price

9) The market value of a quoted company,is known as _______

a) **Market capitalisation**

b) Weighted average price

c) Weighted average price of market capitalisation

d) None of the above

10) Indian primary market ushered in an era of free pricing in_________

a) 1991

b) **1992**

c) 1994

d) 1995

11) _______________ are however required to give full disclosures of the parameters which they had considered while deciding the issue price.

a) **Merchant banker**

b) Company

c) Both a and b

d) SEBI

12) Nowadays, all issues are normally done through the ___________

a) **Book building process**

b) NSE

c) SEBI

d) Merchant banker

13) In case of offer of shares through normal public issue, price is known in _______

a) Book building

b) Market analysis

c) **Advance to investor**

d) Offer Document

14) The actual discovered issue price can be any price in the price band or any price above the floor price. This issue price is called _______________

a) Market price

b) Face value of securities

c) **Cut off price**

d) Base price

15) Floor price is the minimum price at which _______ can be made.

a) **Bid**

b) Sell

c) Purchase

d) None of the above

16) ___________ may contain either the floor price for the securities or a price band within which the investors can bid.

a) Draft offer document

b) **Prospectus**

c) Minutes of meeting

d) Either a or b

17) The spread between the floor and the cap of the price band shall not be more than _________

a) **20%**

b) 30%

c) 15%

d) 10%

18) _________ is the minimum number of days for which a bid should remain open during book building?

a) **3 days**

b) 5 days

c) 8 days

d) 10 days

19) As per SEBI (Issue of Capital and Disclosure Requirements) Regulations, 2009 the Basis of Allotment should be completed within _________ from the issue close date.

a) 3 working days

b) **4 working days**

c) 6 working days

d) 10 working days

20) ASBA is an application containing an authorization to block _________ in the bank account

a) Subscription money

b) Allotment money

c) Call money

d) **Application money**

21) From __________it is mandatory that all public issues are subscribed through ASBA only.

a) **1st January 2016,**

b) 1st January 2019

c) 1st January 2020

d) 1st January 2017

22) It takes _________ after the closure of the book built issue.

a) **6 working days**

b) 8 working days

c) 9 working days

d) 15 working days

23) __________ finalises the list of eligible allottees after deleting the invalid applications

a) **The Registrar**

b) Merchant banker

c) SEBI

d) Corporate CEO

24) ________ coordinates with the Registrar to ensure follow up so that that the flow of applications from collecting bank branches

a) The Registrar

b) Merchant banker

c) **Lead manager**

d) SEBI

25) NSE operates a fully automated screen based bidding system called ________

a) **NEAT IPO**

b) NEAT system

c) NEAT bidding

d) NEAT

26) ____________ will helps investors to evaluate short term and long term prospects of the company.

a) Directors report

b) Annual report

c) **Prospectus**

d) Either a or b

27) Prospectus will be called as ________ in case of a rights issue which is filed with the Registrar of Companies (ROC) and Stock Exchanges (SEs).

a) offer for sale

b) Letter of Offer

c) **Either a or b**

d) Offer document

28) ____________ does not have details of either price or number of shares being offered, or the amount of issue

a) **Red herring prospectus**

b) Abridged Prospectus

c) Either a and b

d) Offer document

29) Lock-in' indicates a____________ for a certain period of time

a) **freeze on the sale of shares**

b) freeze on the application of shares

c) freeze on the allotment of shares

d) freeze on the subscription of shares

30) ADSs are issued by a ___________

a) **Depository bank**

b) Clearing bank

c) RTA

d) Custodian

31) ____________ means a bond issued by an Indian company expressed in foreign currency, and the principal and interest in respect of which is payable in foreign currency'.

a) **Foreign Currency Convertible Bond**

b) ADR

c) GDR

d) All of the above

32) ____________ refers to the legal structure of an exchange whereby the ownership, the management and the trading rights at the exchange are segregated from one another.

a) **Demutualisation**

b) Rematerlistion

c) Both and b

d) None of the above

33) One need to keep ___________ minimum balance of securities in his account with his DP

a) There is no such minimum balance

b) **Zero balance**

c) Minimum 10000

d) Minimum 5000

34) _________ is basically an organisation, which helps register and safeguard the securities of its clients.

a) Custodian

b) Broker

c) **Depositary**

d) Depository participant

35) Demat Request Form (DRF) which is available with the_________ to convert the securities in demat form

a) **DP**

b) SEBI

c) NSE

d) Depository

36) A _________ is a confirmation of trades done on a particular day on behalf of the client by a trading member.

a) **Contract note**

b) Debt instrument

c) Buyers contract

d) Share certificate

37) The maximum brokerage charge by broker is _________

a) 3.5%

b) Minimum not fixed

c) **2.5%**

d) 1.75%

38) _________ facilitates you to lodge your complaint online with SEBI and subsequently view its status.

a) SCORES

b) SEBI Complaints Redress System

c) **Either a or b**

d) Both a and b

39) __________ shares are issued at free of cost to the existing shareholder

a) Right issue

b) **Bonus shares**

c) Preference share

d) Both a and b

e) None of the above

40) __________ bond is issued at discount and redeemed at face value

a) **Zero coupon bond**

b) Convertible bonds

c) Non-convertible bonds

d) Noe of the above

41) __________stock have been overlooked by other investors and which may have a _hidden value'.

a) **Value stock**

b) Growth stock

c) Equity stock

d) Debentures

42) __________ price that you need to know when you have to sell a stock.

a) **Bid price**

b) Ask price

c) Buy

d) Sell

43) __________ is a combination of different investment assets mixed and matched for the purpose of achieving an investor's goal(s)

a) Diversification

b) **Portfolio**

c) Portfolio investment

d) Diversified portfolio

44) _________ refers to the periodic interest payments that are made by the borrower (who is also the issuer of the bond) to the lender

a) Principal

b) **Coupon**

c) Return

d) Borrowings

45) Corporate actions are typically agreed upon by a company's _________

a) Promoters and authorised by the shareholders

b) **Board of Directors and authorised by the shareholders**

c) Board of Directors and authorised by the merchant bankers

d) Authorised by SEBI

46) _________ gives the relationship between the current price of a stock and the dividend paid by its issuing company during the last 12 months.

a) Dividend yield

b) Dividend return

c) Interest

d) Yield to maturity

47) _________ reduce the number of shares outstanding in the market.

a) Stock split

b) Stock consolidation

c) **Buyback of shares**

d) Allotment of shares

48) Auction settlement can be done within _________ period

a) T+2 working days

b) **T+3 working days**

c) T+4 working days

d) T+6 working days

49) The first day of the no-delivery period is the __________
a) **Ex- date**

b) Ex- dividend

c) Ex- delivery

d) No delivery period

50) __________ is an alternative dispute resolution mechanism provided by a stock exchange
a) **Arbitration**

b) Investor redressal cell

c) SCORES

d) All of the above

Define the following

1. Primary market
2. Equity share
3. Right issue
4. Bonus share
5. Issue price
6. IPO
7. Cut-off Price
8. Demutualisation
9. Depository participant
10. Custodia
11. Buyback of shares
12. Dividend

Short question (Write your answer into 20-30 words)

1. What is the role of the primary market?
2. What do you mean by face value of shares?
3. What is the main difference between offer of shares through book building and offer of shares through a normal public issue?
4. What is the role of registrar?
5. What is the difference between private and public issue

6.   What is the contract note?

7.   What are the factor that will affect the price of the stock

8.   What is the rolling settlement?

9.   What is meant by dividend declared by the company

10. Explain the difference between stock split and stock consolidated

Short question (Write your answer into 30-50 words)

1.   Why do companies need to issue shares to the public?

2.   What are the differant kinds of issues ?

3.   Distinguish between private and public limited company

4.   What do you mean by prospectus and explain its features

5.   What is the role of the secondary market?

6.   What is the screen based trading system? Explain its features

7.   Explain the term bonds with its features

8.   Explain types of bonds?

9.   Explain the difference between Growth Stock and value stock?

10. What do you mean by diversification and explain its benefits?

Long questions

1.   What precautions one has to take before investing in the stock market ?

2.   What are the sources available to investors for redressing the grievances?

3.   What are the products dealt in the secondary market?

4.   If you want to become owner of the company in which security you will invest and why?

5.   Being an individual you will start any company and if you want to raise the funds, what securities will you use for it ?

Unit 3
Mutual Fund Products and Features

Meaning

What is the mutual fund

A mutual fund is a company that pools money from many investors and invests the money in securities such as stocks, bonds, and short-term debt.

Features:-

1) *Diversification*

One of the most prominent advantages of investing in mutual funds is diversification. It is the process of spreading a given investment over multiple assets classes. Diversification helps us create an assorted portfolio that segregates the headwinds experienced in various sectors. Money is invested in a mixture of assets according to one's risk appetite.

2) *Professional Management*

A lot of investors do not have the time or resources to conduct their research and purchase individual stocks. This is where professional management becomes quite useful. Several people invest in mutual funds for the professional expertise it provides to one's investments. A fund manager continuously monitors investments and adjusts the portfolio accordingly to meet its objectives.

3) *Tax Benefits*

The tax benefits associated with a particular kind of mutual fund is perhaps what draws most investors to this investment vehicle. To encourage investments in mutual funds, the Government of India offers several tax benefits.

4) _Highly Liquid_

One can easily sell mutual funds to meet their financial needs. Upon liquidation, the money is deposited in your bank account in a few days. Additionally, there are mutual funds that provide faster disbursal. They are called funds having instant redemption facility , wherein the money is transferred to your bank on the same day.

5) _Easy Investment_

It is very easy to invest in mutual funds, i.e. you can do this either online or offline. You simply need to visit your Asset Management Company (AMC)(discussed in a later part) website and submit the necessary documents to start on your investment journey. Moreover, you can also visit your AMC in person and sign the physical documents to get started. This ease of investment makes mutual funds are preferable avenue.

Structure of Mutual Fund

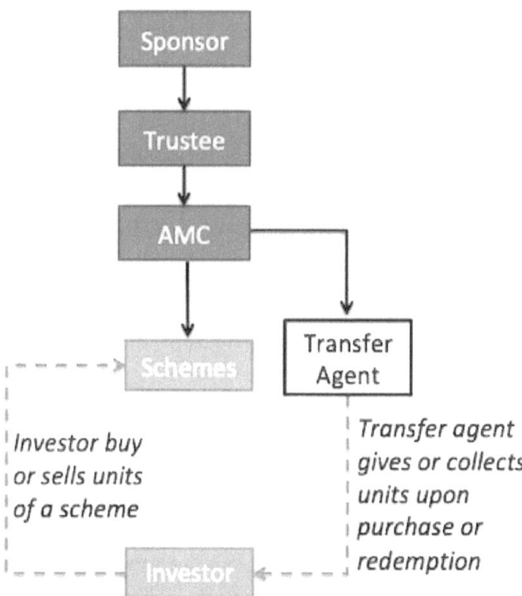

It is SEBI who has prepared the framework of the above 3-tier structure of mutual funds. All mutual funds operate in India under SEBI guidelines.

**It is the SPONSORS (also called promoters) who first conceptualised the idea of starting a mutual fund business.** Before they can act further, they must approach SEBI for registration of the business.

Which are the credentials required?

- The sponsor must have experience of **5 years in financial services.**
- They must be a profit making company (3 out of 5 years).
- Last 5 years the net worth of the company must be positive.
- Has profits after depreciation, interest and tax in three of out the five preceding years including the fifth year
- The sponsor has contributed / contributes not less than 40% of the net worth of the asset management company

Once the certification is received, further steps can be taken to start a mutual fund activity. Which are the next steps?

1. Formation of Trust.
2. Appointment of AMC.
3. Appointment of Depository (Custodian), Registrar, Transfer Agent, and Auditor.

Once approved by SEBI, the sponsor creates a Public Trust (the Second tier) as per the Indian Trusts Act, 1882.

Trustee

Trusts have no legal identity in India and cannot enter into contracts, *hence the Trustees are the people authorised to act on behalf of the Trust.*

Contracts are entered into in the name of the Trustees. Once the Trust is created, it is registered with SEBI after which this trust is known as the mutual fund.

It is important to understand the difference between the Sponsor and the Trust. They are two separate entities.

Sponsor is not the Trust; i.e. Sponsor is not the Mutual Fund. It is the Trust which is the Mutual Fund. The Trustees role is not to manage the money. Their job is only to see whether the money is being managed as per stated objectives. Trustees may be seen as the internal regulators of a mutual fund.

Who manages investors money

- This is the *role of the Asset Management Company (the Third tier)*.
- Trustees appoint the Asset Management Company (AMC), to manage investor's money.

- The *AMC in return charges a fee for the services* provided and this *fee is borne by the investors as it is deducted from the money collected from them.*

- The *AMC's Board of Directors must have at least 50% directors,* who are not associate of, or associated in any manner with, the sponsor or any of its subsidiaries or the trustees.

- The AMC has to *be approved by SEBI.* The AMC functions *under the supervision of its Board of Directors, and also under the direction of the Trustees and SEBI.*

- It is the AMC, which in the name of the Trust, floats and manages schemes by buying and selling securities.

- In order to do this, *the AMC needs to follow all rules and regulations prescribed by SEBI and as per the Investment Management Agreement it* signs with the Trustees. Whenever the fund intends to launch a new scheme, the AMC has to submit a Draft Offer Document to SEBI.

- This draft offer document, *after getting SEBI approval becomes the offer document of the scheme.*

- The *Offer Document (OD) is a legal document and investors rely upon the information provided in the OD for investing in the mutual fund scheme.*

- The *Compliance Officer has to sign the Due Diligence Certificate* in the OD.

- This certificate says that *all the information provided inside the OD is true and correct.*

- This ensures that there is accountability and somebody's responsible for the OD.

- In case *there is no compliance officer, then senior executives like CEO, Chairman of the AMC has to sign the due diligence certificate.*

- The certificate ensures *that the AMC takes responsibility of the OD and its contents.*

Who is custodian

Meaning

A mutual fund custodian is a financial institution, such as a bank or trust company, that holds and safeguards the securities of a mutual fund. Custodians are responsible for keeping the investment account of the mutual fund. The assets of the mutual fund scheme are held by the custodian.

- A custodian's role is safe keeping of physical securities and also keeping a tab on the corporate actions like rights, bonus and dividends declared by the companies in which the fund has invested.

- The Custodian *is appointed by the Board of Trustees.* Since the custody of the assets is separated from the management it protects the investors against fraud and misappropriation.

- The custodian also *participates in a clearing and settlement system through approved depository companies on behalf of mutual funds, in case of dematerialized securities.*

- In India today, *securities (and units of mutual funds) are no longer held in physical form but in dematerialized form with the Depositories.*

- The holdings are held *in the Depository through Depository Participants (DPs).* Only the physical securities are held by the Custodian.

- The deliveries and *receipt of units of a mutual fund are done by the custodian or a depository participant at the instruction* of the AMC and under the overall direction and responsibility of the Trustees.

- Regulations provide that the Sponsor and the Custodian must be separate entities.

Difference between AMC and custodian

For example; HDFC *AMC is the Asset Management Company for HDFC Mutual Fund.* Custodian – The custodian *has the custody of all the shares and various other securities bought by the AMC.* The custodian is responsible for the safekeeping of all the securities.

Difference between AMC and Trustee

An asset management company (AMC) manages the funds raised from the investors, but it is required to appoint mutual fund trustees who will act independently to protect unit holders' interests. Trustees must regularly review the AMC's operations to make sure there are no violations.

What is the role of AMC

An *asset management company (AMC) manages the funds raised from the investors,* but it is required to appoint mutual fund trustees who will act independently to protect unitholders' interests. Trustees must regularly review the AMC's operations to make sure there are no violations.

- The role of the AMC is to manage investor's money on a day to day basis. Thus it is imperative that people with the highest integrity are involved with this activity.

- The AMC cannot deal with a single broker beyond a certain limit of transactions.

- The AMC cannot act as a Trustee for some other Mutual Fund. The responsibility of preparing the OD lies with the AMC.

- Appointments of intermediaries like independent financial advisors (IFAs), national and regional distributors, banks, etc. is also done by the AMC.

Finally, it is the AMC which is responsible for the acts of its employees and service providers. As can be seen, it is the AMC that does all the operations. All activities by the AMC are done under the name of the Trust, i.e. the mutual fund.

The AMC charges a fee for providing its services. SEBI has prescribed limits for this. This fee is borne by the investor as the fee is charged to the scheme, in fact, the fee is charged as a percentage of the scheme's net assets.

An important point to note here is that this fee is included in the overall expenses permitted by SEBI.

There is a maximum limit to the amount that can be charged as expense to the scheme, and this fee has to be within that limit. Thus regulations ensure that beyond a certain limit, investor's money is not used for meeting expenses.

OR

Role of AMC

1. *Research and Analysis*

Portfolio construction requires in depth analysis of which asset class to pick depending on the prevailing market condition. Analysts in an AMC would conduct in-depth market analysis both from micro and macro level perspective.

2. *Portfolio Construction*

The portfolio construction is done by defining the investment objective or rationale. The main aim of a fund manager is to generate more returns than the benchmark. The fund managers would take the market findings of AMC's analyst and would start crafting a fund scheme.

3. *Asset Allocation*

At this stage, the mutual fund objective is fixed. Now the asset has to be allocated based on the investment rationale, like for deb based fund not more than 20% to be allocated in equities, etc. Post the broad asset class allocation, the process now boils down to selecting real assets like for equity based ◆ growth fund, which all growth stocks to fit in large cap so that desired return can be achieved.

4. *Performance Review*

The AMC would continuously monitor the performance of the fund scheme. As it is essential to be a better performer than the competitors in the market.

What is the New Fund Offer

- Once the 3 – tier structure is in place, the AMC launches new schemes, under the name of the Trust, after getting approval from the Trustees and SEBI.

- The launch of a new scheme is known as a New Fund Offer (NFO). We see NFOs coming up in markets regularly. It is like an invitation to the investors to put their money into the mutual fund scheme by subscribing to its units.

- When a scheme is launched, the distributors talk to potential investors and collect money from them by way of cheques or demand drafts.

- Mutual funds cannot accept cash. (Mutual funds units can also be purchased on-line through a number of intermediaries who offer on-line purchase / redemption facilities).

- Before investing, it is expected that the investor reads the Offer Document (OD) carefully to understand the risks associated with the scheme.

A New Fund Offer refers to the inception of a new mutual fund scheme. During an NFO, the fund house invites investors to subscribe to the units of the new scheme. This is the initial phase when the fund is open for investment, and it typically has a fixed subscription period, after which the NFO closes, and regular trading begins.

Types of NFO

New Fund Offer (NFO) can be classified into three main types based on the structure and features of the mutual fund schemes:

1. Open-ended

Open-ended funds are those mutual fund schemes *in which you can invest or redeem at any time.* The open-ended fund provides high liquidity as you can enter or exit the scheme anytime.

Even after the NFO period is over, you can purchase units of open-ended funds at the prevailing market Net Asset Value (NAV) on any business day.

2. Closed-Ended

You can invest during the NFO period only. These schemes are issued for a fixed tenure. Once the NFO period is over, further investments in the fund are not allowed. Redemption happens after the funds get listed on the stock exchange. *As per the SEBI rule, all closed-end funds must be listed on the exchange.*

3. Interval Funds

Interval funds represent the *characteristics of both open-ended funds and close-ended funds.* These funds fall under the category of closed-ended funds, but they allow you to make purchases and redemptions through the AMC window at regular intervals. *These intervals may occur annually or semi-annually, allowing investors to transact within specific timeframes.*

✖ Benefits of NFO

1. **Fresh Investment Opportunity:** NFOs introduce a new mutual fund scheme, allowing investors to get in at the fund's inception. This can be appealing to those who want to start with a clean slate and be part of the fund's journey from the beginning.

2. **Low Initial Investment:** NFO units are typically offered at a fixed price, often set at Rs 10 per unit. This makes NFOs accessible to investors with a modest budget, as they can start with a relatively low initial investment.

3. **Unique Investment Themes:** Some NFOs bring innovative or specialised investment themes or strategies to the market, providing investors with the chance to diversify their portfolios in a distinct way.

4. **Opportunity to Capitalise on Future Performance:** If the NFO is managed effectively and its investment strategy aligns with your financial goals, you may benefit from the fund's performance as it grows over time.

5. **<u>Professional Management:</u>** NFOs are managed by experienced fund managers who make investment decisions based on the fund's objectives and market conditions, potentially enhancing the chances of achieving your investment goals.

Registrar and Transfer agent

A registrar and transfer agent (RTA) is responsible for keeping track of investor transactions in mutual funds. RTAs also serve as the main point of contact for mutual fund investors.

Role of RTA

- *Keeping records*

RTAs are responsible for keeping records of all transactions, including buying, redeeming, switching in or out, and changing bank mandates.

- *Acting as custodians*

RTAs are responsible for keeping investor records accurate, transparent, and compliant.

- *Processing transactions*

RTAs process transactions involving securities, such as issuing and cancelling certificates to reflect changes in ownership.

- *Providing services*

RTAs assist with various investor services, such as handling queries, providing account statements, and other investor services

How to invest in New Fund Offer

Investing in a New Fund Offering can be *<u>done through both offline and online modes, but a crucial step before investing is ensuring completion of your KYC (Know Your Customer) process.</u>*

This verification is essential, as an NFO application from a KYC non-compliant investor may be rejected. Let's explore the two modes separately:

<u>Investing in NFOS - Offline Mode:</u> In the offline mode, you fill out a physical form and sign it with your folio number (if your are an existing investor with the fund house) and other details, following KYC verification. In case you are not an existing investor of the fund house you will have to submit a fresh application for the NFO and post unit allocation, folio number will be allotted.

1. Offline investments in NFOs are usually facilitated through brokers or directly at the Asset Management Company (AMC) office, where the AMC guides you through the process.

2. If using an authorised broker, submit the form, cheque, and other details to the broker. Brokers often double as financial advisors, assisting with fund selection and SIP structuring.

3. Existing folio holders with the AMC can utilise their folio number, streamlining the application process.

4. Complete the offline form, verify details, sign, and submit it to the broker along with the NFO payment cheque.

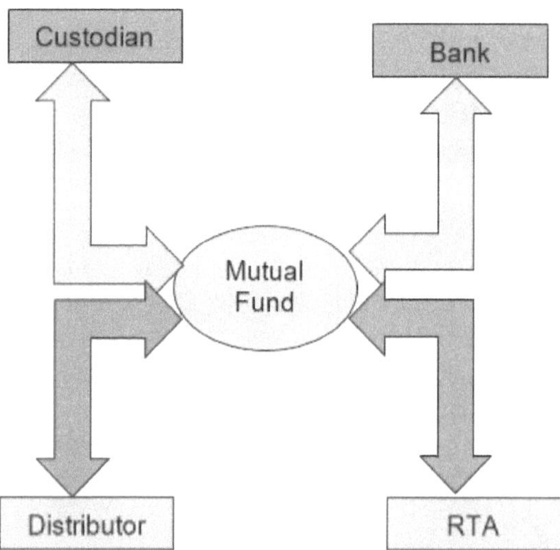

Investing in NFOS - Online Mode: In the online mode, you fill out the NFO application on the internet, checking your KYC status before proceeding with the Investment.

Log in or register to your platform using your unique credentials.

1. Browse available NFOS on the website or through your online broker, who typically provides all NFO investment details.

2. Select the preferred fund, determine the investment amount based on your allocation plan, and use online resources for guidance.

3. Enter the investment amount and specify whether it's a lump sum or SIP investment.

Rights and obligation of investors of investors

Mutual funds in India are regulated by The Securities and Exchange Board of India (SEBI). One of the primary responsibilities of SEBI is protection of investor interests. Every mutual fund investor enjoys rights under SEBI's regulations. Asset Management Companies are obligated to ensure that every investor is able to exercise his / her rights. Below are some of the key rights of investors in India.

1) Go through Scheme Related Documents before investing

An investor has the right to go through all the scheme related documents before investing. These documents *include the Scheme Information Document, Statement of Additional Information and Key Information Memorandum.* We have discussed some major items in the contents of these documents in our chapter 'SID, SAI, KIM before investing'. The AMC must provide **these documents to investors if asked for.** If there are any changes in a scheme, the *AMC must also inform unit-holders / investors of the scheme about the changes.*

2) Know commissions paid to distributors

If you are investing through a mutual fund distributor or financial advisor, *then you have the right to know the commissions paid to the distributor on your mutual fund investments. From 2016, SEBI has mandated that AMCs disclose actual commissions paid to distributors for each scheme in half yearly (September / March) Consolidated Account Statement (CAS).* This will give a fair idea if your advisor has your best interests in mind when recommending mutual fund schemes for investments.

3) Interest on delayed dividends

If your mutual fund scheme declares dividends then the dividend amount should get credited to your bank account *within 30 days from the date of dividend declaration.* If the AMC is not able to credit the dividend amount to your bank account within 30 days, *then it is liable to pay you interest at the rate of 15% per annum for the period of delay.*

4) Interest on delayed redemption

If you redeem units of your mutual fund scheme, then the redemption proceeds should get credited to your bank account **within 10 days from the date when redemption instruction was processed.** If the AMC is not able to credit the dividend amount to your bank account within 30 days, then it is liable to pay you interest at the rate of 15% per annum for the period of delay.

5) Consolidated Account Statement

A CAS details all the transactions and investor's holding at the end of the month including transaction charges paid to the distributor, across all schemes of all mutual funds, by an investor. A **CAS for each calendar month is issued to the investors in whose folios transactions have taken place during that month**. A CAS every half yearly (September/ March) is issued, detailing holding at the end of the six month, across all schemes of all mutual funds, to all such investors in whose folios no transaction has taken place during that period.

6) Complaint redressal system

If you have a complaint on any investment related issue, you can contact the grievance cell of the concerned Asset Management Company. Every *AMC must have a grievance cell or grievance redressal officer.* The *contact details of the grievance cell* should be mentioned on the AMC's website. Investors can also **register their complaints with Trustees** of the mutual fund. The names of Trustees of a fund are mentioned in the Statement of Additional Information. If your complaint is not satisfactorily resolved by AMC or trustees of the fund, then you can send your complaint to SEBI as per rights of investors under SEBI.

Equity oriented Fund

An equity fund *is a mutual fund scheme that invests predominantly in equity stocks.* In the Indian context, as per current SEBI Mutual Fund Regulations, *an equity mutual fund scheme must invest at least 65% of the scheme's assets in equities and equity related instruments.*

- Equity funds account for around 30% of the total AUM managed by mutual funds.

- An Equity Fund can be actively managed or passively managed. Index funds and ETFs are passively managed.

- Equity mutual funds are principally categorised according to company size, the investment style of the holdings in the portfolio and geography.

- The size of an equity fund is determined by a market capitalization, while the investment style, reflected in the fund's stock holdings, is also used to categorise equity mutual funds.

- Equity funds are also categorised by whether they are domestic (investing in stocks of only Indian companies) or international (investing in stocks of overseas companies). These can be broad market, regional or single-country funds.

- Some specialty equity funds target business sectors, such as health care, commodities and real estate and are known as Sectoral Funds.

Definition of equity fund

Equity oriented Funds are funds that invest the investor's money in equity and related instruments of companies.

Section 115 T of the Income Tax Act, 1961 lays down that equity oriented fund means such fund where the investible funds are invested by way of equity shares in domestic companies to the extent of more than 65% of the total proceeds of such fund. In case of equity funds investors need not pay long term capital gains. Hence it is important that this investment norm is met by the fund.

The different types of mutual funds based on their asset classes are as follows:

1. ***Equity funds:*** Equity funds mainly invest their assets in the shares of companies. As per the guidelines, an equity mutual fund scheme should invest at least 65% of its assets in equities or equity-related investments. The remaining funds are invested in other, more secure asset classes to offset the risk. The returns from these funds depend on the performance of the shares they invest.

Equity funds can be again categorised in many ways, such as:

- Based on the way they are managed - active and passive funds.

- Based on the market capitalisation of the stocks they invest in - small-, mid-, multi-, and large-cap funds.

- Based on their geography - domestic and foreign funds. They can also be classified as broad-market, regional or single-country funds.

Based on the sector they invest in - pharma, FMCG, real estate, etc.

- Equity funds are suitable for those who have long investment horizons. Furthermore, they have a track record of providing superior returns than other types of mutual funds, making them a solid option for building wealth.

2. ***Debt funds:*** Debt funds invest their assets in fixed-income instruments, such as corporate/government bonds, T-bills, or certificates of deposits. Compared to equity funds, debt funds are less risky and have lower expense ratios. Moreover, they give better returns than traditional investment options like fixed deposits. Hence, they can be a better choice for those seeking regular income.

3. ***Hybrid funds:*** Hybrid funds consist of both debt and equity components. This type of mutual fund is suitable for investors with

a moderate risk appetite. Hybrid funds can be classified based on their asset allocation as follows:

- *Conservative hybrid funds* - invest at least 75% of the asset in debt and the rest in equity.

- *Aggressive hybrid funds* - invest 65% to 80% of the asset in equity or equity-related instruments and the remaining in money market and debt instruments.

- *Dynamic asset allocation funds* - invest in both debt and equity, and their proportion varies with the market condition.

- *Multi-asset allocation funds* - invest at least 10% of their money in at least 3 asset classes, and the proportion changes with market conditions.

- *Arbitrage funds* - invest a minimum of 65% of their asset in equity and the rest in debt and money market instruments.

- *Equity savings funds* - invest at least 65% of their asset in equity and equity-related instruments and a minimum of 10% in debt instruments.

4. ***Money market funds:*** Money market funds normally invest in low-risk, short-term securities such as T-bills, certificates of deposit, commercial paper, etc. They offer high liquidity; investors often invest in the funds as a short-term cash management tool.

The average maturity of a money market fund is one year

What is open and close ended scheme

1. Equity Funds (or any Mutual Fund scheme for that matter) can either be open ended or close ended.

2. An open ended scheme allows the investor to enter and exit at his convenience, anytime (except under certain conditions) whereas a ***close ended scheme restricts the freedom of entry and exit.***

3. Whenever a new fund is launched by an AMC, it is known as New Fund Offer (NFO). ***Units are offered to investors at the par value of Rs. 10/ unit.***

4. In case of open ended schemes, ***investors can buy the units even after the NFO period is over.*** Thus, when the fund sells units, the investor buys the units from the fund and when the investor wishes to redeem the units, the fund repurchases the units from the investor. This can be done even after the NFO has closed. ***The buy***

/ sell of units takes place at the Net Asset Value (NAV) declared by the fund.

5. The freedom to invest after the NFO period is over is not there in close ended schemes. Investors have to invest only during the NFO period; i.e. as long as the NFO is on or the scheme is open for subscription. Once the NFO closes, new investors cannot enter, nor can existing investors exit, till the term of the scheme comes to an end.

    a) However, **in order to provide entry and exit options, close ended mutual funds** list their schemes on stock exchanges. This provides an opportunity for investors to buy and sell the units from each other.

    b) This is just like buying / selling shares on the stock exchange. This is done through a stock broker. The **outstanding units of the fund does not increase in this case since the fund is itself not selling any units.**

6) Sometimes, close ended funds also offer buy-back of fund shares / units , thus offering another avenue for investors to exit the fund. Therefore, regulations drafted in India permit investors in close ended funds to exit even before the term is over.

➡ *Index Fund*

An index fund is a portfolio of stocks or bonds designed to mimic the composition and performance of a financial market index. Index funds have lower expenses and fees than actively managed funds. Index funds follow a passive investment strategy.

➡ *Tracking Error*

Tracking error is a financial performance measure that shows how closely an investment portfolio's return fluctuations match those of a benchmark. It's often used in the context of mutual funds, hedge funds, or exchange-traded funds (ETFs).

(This can be easily calculated on a standard MS office spreadsheet, by taking the daily returns of the Index, the daily returns of the NAV of the scheme, finding the difference between the two for each day and then calculating the standard deviation of difference by using the excel formula for standard deviation)

Tracking error is the standard deviation of returns over time. It's calculated by subtracting the returns of an index fund from its target index and then finding the annualised standard deviation of that difference.

Factors that can affect a portfolio's tracking error include:

- The number of stocks in the portfolio
- Differences in market capitalization, investment style, and timing
- Changes in index constituents
- Corporate actions
- Market volatility
- Interest rates

For example, if the XYZ Fund is supposed to track the Big Stock Index and the Big Stock Index returns 10% while the XYZ Fund returns 9.7%, the difference of 9.7% - 10% = -0.3% is the tracking error.

Cap refers to market capitalization. *Market capitalization refers to aggregate valuation of the company based on the current market price and the number of shares issued.* Accordingly companies are classified into

- Large cap companies– typically the top 100 to 200 stocks which feature in Nifty 50
- Mid cap companies– Stocks below large cap which belong to the mid cap segment
- **Small cap companies – Typically stocks with market capitalization of less than Rs. 5000 cr.**

What are Diversified large Cap Funds?

Large cap diversified funds invest in companies with a market capitalization of at least Rs. 20,000 crore. These funds generally **invest in shares of popular blue chip companies.** The Nifty index is the benchmark used by large cap diversified equity mutual funds.

Large cap funds offer diversification across multiple sectors, reducing the impact of sector-specific risks. The goal of these funds is to generate capital appreciation over the long term.

Large cap funds restrict their stock selection to the large cap stocks. *It is generally perceived that large cap stocks are those which have sound businesses, strong management, globally competitive products and are quick to respond to market dynamics.* Therefore, diversified large cap funds are considered as stable and safe. The stocks command high liquidity.

These funds are *actively managed funds unlike the index funds which are passively managed,* In an actively managed fund the fund manager pores over data and information, researches the company, the economy, analyses market trends, takes into account government policies on different sectors and then selects the stock to invest

A point to be noted here is that anything other than index funds are actively managed funds and they _generally have higher expenses as compared to index funds._ In this case, the fund manager has the choice to invest in stocks beyond the index. Thus, active decision making comes in.

Any scheme which is involved in active decision making is incurring higher expenses and may also be assuming higher risks. This is mainly because as the stock selection universe increases from index stocks to large caps to midcaps and finally to small caps, the risk levels associated with each category increases above the previous category.

The logical Points to Remember from this is that _actively managed funds should also deliver higher returns than the index, as investors must be compensated for higher risks._ But this is not always so. Studies have shown that a _majority of actively managed funds are unable to beat the index returns on a consistent basis year after year._ Secondly, there is no guaranteeing which actively managed fund will beat the index in a given year. Index funds therefore have grown exponentially in some countries due to the inconsistency of returns of actively managed funds.

Mid cap funds

- Midcap funds invest in stocks belonging to the mid cap segment of the market.

- Many of these midcaps _are said to be the emerging blue chips' or tomorrow's large caps'._

- There can be actively managed or passively managed mid cap funds.

- There are indices such as the **CNX Midcap index which tracks the midcap segment** of the markets and there are some passively managed index funds investing in the CNX Midcap companies.

Features

- _Growth potential:_ Mid-cap stocks tend to offer investors greater growth potential than large cap stocks.

- _Volatility:_ Mid-cap stocks are less volatile than small cap stocks.

- _Performance:_ From November 1991 through September 2023, mid-caps outperform both large- and small-caps.

➡ *Sectoral Funds*

A sectoral fund is a type of investment fund *that invests in a specific industry or sector.* They can be mutual funds or exchange-traded funds (ETFs).

Funds that invest in stocks from a single sector or related sectors are called Sectoral funds. Examples of such funds are Banking Funds, IT Funds, Pharma Funds, Infrastructure Funds, etc. **Regulations do not permit funds to invest over 10% of their Net Asset Value in a single company**

Sectoral funds are *also known as specialty funds.* They are *equity funds that invest in companies in certain segments of the economy.* Sectoral funds *are riskier than diversified funds because they lack diversification across sectors.* This means that your investment could suffer significant losses if the chosen sector underperforms or faces challenges.

✳ *Here are some features of sectoral funds:*

a) *Volatility*

Sectoral funds are more volatile because they focus on only one area of the economy, therefore they have no diversification.

b) *Risk*

Sectoral funds are one of the riskiest investments because they are subject to market volatility and carry market risks.

c) *Exposure*

Sectoral funds can help you pursue growth, diversify your portfolio, and manage risks.

✳ *Other Equity Schemes*

1) *Arbitrage Funds*

These invest simultaneously in the cash and the derivatives market and take advantage of the price differential of a stock in the cash and derivative segment by taking opposite positions in the two markets

(For Example:-The company's stock might sell at $20 per share today, but the majority of investors may feel it is primed for a spike next month. In that case, a futures contract with a one-month maturity date may be valued much more highly. The difference between the cash and futures price for ABC stock is called the arbitrage profit.)

2) Multi cap funds

As the name suggests, Multi Cap Funds invest their corpus in a portfolio of equity and equity-related stocks of companies with varying market capitalizations. So, in a Multi Cap fund, you will find investments in large-cap, small-cap, and mid-cap companies. The fund manager has total freedom to invest in any stock from any sector.

3) Quant funds

In the case of these funds quantitative models are used for stock selection and allocation of weights based on company's size, financial performance and liquidity.

International Equity funds

International equity funds are mutual funds or exchange-traded funds (ETFs) that invest in stocks of companies located in other countries. They can help investors to access a variety of global investment opportunities and reduce the impact of domestic market fluctuations

This can be a Fund of Fund, _whereby, we invest in one fund, which acts as a _feeder' fund for some other fund(s),_ .i.e invests in other mutual funds, or it can be a fund which directly invests in overseas equities.

International funds _can help investors diversify their portfolios and avoid missing out on global opportunities._ They can also help investors earn steady returns, even if the Indian economy faces a downturn

Growth funds

Growth funds are a type of mutual fund that invest in growth stocks to achieve capital appreciation.

They focus on companies that have significant potential for above-average revenue and earnings growth.

Growth funds are diversified portfolios of stocks that primarily aim at capital appreciation over time. They typically have minimal or nil payouts of dividends.

Growth funds are different from dividend funds because the NAV of a growth option will always be higher than the dividend option. This is because the profits are reinvested in the growth option and may grow in value over time. (They focus on companies that are experiencing significant earnings or revenue growth, rather than companies that pay out dividends)

➡ *ELSS*

Equity Linked Savings Scheme (ELSS) funds are tax-saving mutual funds in India. These investments combine the benefits of equity investments with tax deductions under Section 80C. These ELSS schemes come with a 3-year lock-in period.

ELSS or Equity Linked Savings Schemes are Mutual fund investment schemes that help you save income tax. That's why they are also known as tax-saving funds. The Income Tax Act, under section 80c, allows taxpayers to invest up to INR 1.5 lakh in specific securities and claim it as a deduction from their taxable income.

However it must be noted that investors cannot, under any circumstances, get their money back before 3 years from the date of investment.

➡ *Funds of Fund*

These are funds which do not directly invest in stocks and shares but invest in units of other mutual funds which in their opinion will perform well and give high returns. Almost all mutual funds offer fund of funds schemes.

➡ *Basic offer Document*

A document containing the details of a particular mutual scheme offered by an Asset Management Company (AMC) to the public for investing is known as a mutual fund offer document or a prospectus.

This document comprises two parts - *the Scheme Information Document (SID) and the Statement of Additional Information (SAI).*

  a) *The Scheme Information Document consists of important information regarding the scheme such as the investment objective, the pattern of asset allocation, risk involved, investment approach, fund manager, benchmark index, fees and expenses, etc.*

  b) The Statement of Additional Information, on the other hand, carries all statutory information of the mutual fund house.

The preparation of both the SID and SAI *are done in the format prescribed by the Securities and Exchange Board of India (SEBI)* and they have to be submitted to SEBI. The fund house can also include any disclosures that it feels is necessary for the investor.

✖ *How to read the mutual fund offer documents?*

Since the SID contains important details of the scheme, it is imperative to go through it thoroughly. While doing so, ensure that you read the below-mentioned points in the SID:

1) *Investment objective -*

This section explains the intent behind the launch of a scheme and how it will be achieved. The investment objective clarifies the doubt investors may have concerning the names of the schemes. For instance, 'Capital Protection Oriented Funds' may not guarantee protection of capital and hence, the investment objective clears such ambiguities.

2) *Asset Allocation -*

This section indicates how the scheme will allot its assets to the relevant asset classes (such as debt, equity, and gold) under usual market conditions. The pattern of asset allocation indicates the range of the maximum and minimum exposure to the various asset classes. Investors can judge if a scheme is debt-oriented, equity-oriented, commodity-oriented, etc., from the asset allocation and give them an idea whether the scheme fits their investment requirements or not.

3) *Investment strategy -*

This section explains the approach or style the fund house will follow while choosing the securities to invest in. This is vital because the investment strategy is a reflection of the systems and processes the fund house follows. Fund houses with a clear investment strategy impart a sense of confidence in the minds of investors.

4) *Benchmark of the scheme -*

A benchmark is chosen for a particular mutual fund scheme so as to structure the scheme according to the constituents of the benchmark.

5) *Risk factors -*

Mutual funds carry certain risks with them which can hamper the valuation of the investments. Investors should be aware of the various types of risks that the scheme carries so that they can evaluate if they can tolerate the risks for the achievement of capital appreciation.

6) *Fund manager -*

The expertise of the fund manager is crucial for the scheme's overall performance in the long run. A few of the qualities that you should look for in the fund manager are the experience, qualification, track record, etc. This information can be found highlighted in the SID.

7) *Past performance -*

Though the past performance of a fund cannot guarantee its future performance, it can be used to guide your investment decision. The SID of an existing mutual fund scheme will bear the scheme's past performance over different time frames. This information can be used to assess if the track record clocked by a particular fund fulfils the investment objective of the fund.

8) *Fees and expenses -*

The expenses charged by the AMC are directly proportional to the net returns delivered by a particular scheme. In the process of fetching optimal returns for the investor, the AMC will levy charges in the form of loads, fund management fees, switching charges, etc. These charges are deducted from the NAV of the scheme and hence, as an investor you should look for a scheme that has a lower expense ratio which would translate to you achieving higher capital gains.

9) *Investment options -*

Most mutual fund schemes offer 2 options of investment - growth and dividend. The dividend option further offers a payout and reinvestment option. Also, there are various modes of investing such as the SIP (Systematic Investment Plan), lump-sum investment, and STP (Systematic Transfer Plan). Remember to read through the SID to look for these options so that you can make an informed decision based on your investment needs.

What is a Key Information Memorandum?

A KIM or Key Information Memorandum is the condensed form of the SID and contains the essential components of the offer document. The KIM contains the following information:

- Details of the AMC and the scheme such as the mutual fund's name, its AMC and Trustees, etc.

- Details of the scheme such as the inception date, issue date, investment objective, risk profile, name of the fund manager, benchmark index, etc.

- Options and plans offered by the scheme

- Minimum investment details

- Scheme's past performance over various time frames
- Loads and recurring expenses
- Contact details of RTA (Registrar and Transfer Agent)
- Comparison with other existing schemes

✖ *What is the Net Asset Value*

NAV full form stands for Net Asset Value. It represents the market value per unit for a particular mutual fund. It is calculated by deducting the liabilities from total asset value divided by the number of units.

One needs to gather the market value of a portfolio and divide it by the total current fund unit number to determine the price of each fund unit.

Most of the time, the unit cost of **mutual funds** begin with Rs. 10 and increase as the asset under the funds grow. Going by this rule, the more popular a mutual fund is, the higher is its NAV.

The calculation of the net value is pretty straightforward. One can easily do it by using the NAV formula below–

Net Value of an Asset = (Total Asset – Total Liabilities)/ Total Outstanding Shares

However, it is crucial to input the correct qualifying items under assets and liabilities to get an accurate net value of assets.

➡ **Fund Fact Sheet**

After an investor has entered into a scheme, he must monitor his investments regularly. This can be achieved by going through the Fund Fact Sheet. This is a monthly document which all mutual funds have to publish. This document gives all details as regards

- The AUMs of all its schemes
- Top holdings in all the portfolios of all the schemes • loads, minimum investment • performance over 1, 3, 5 years and also since launch
- Comparison of scheme's performance with the benchmark index (most mutual fund schemes compare their performance with a benchmark index such as the Nifty 50) over the same time periods
- Fund managers outlook
- Portfolio composition
- Expense ratio

- Portfolio turnover

- Risk adjusted returns

- Equity/ debt split for schemes

- YTM for debt portfolios and other information which the mutual fund considers important from the investor's decision making point of view.

Expenses Ratio

Mutual fund *fees and expenses are charges that may be incurred by investors who hold mutual funds.* Operating a mutual fund involves *costs, including shareholder transaction costs, investment advisory fees, and marketing and distribution expenses.* Funds pass along these costs to investors in several ways.

Some funds impose "shareholder fees" directly on investors whenever they buy or sell shares.

In addition, every fund has regular, recurring, fund-wide "operating expenses". Funds typically pay their operating expenses out of fund assets— which means that investors indirectly pay these costs.

Although they may seem negligible, fees and expenses can substantially reduce an investor's earnings when the investment is held for a long period of time.

For the reasons cited above, it is important for a prospective investor to compare the fees of the various funds under consideration. Investors should also compare fees against industry benchmarks and averages. There are many different types of fees, as discussed below. To facilitate the comparison of funds, it is helpful to compare the total expense ratio. The following table shows the weighted average total expense ratios for different types of mutual funds organised in the United States as of December 31, 2020, as published by Morningstar,

Expense Ratio (meaning)

An expense ratio is the annual maintenance fee that mutual funds charge to cover their expenses.

It's calculated by dividing the total expenses of the mutual fund by the value of assets under management (AUM). The expense ratio includes components such as:

- Fund manager's fee

- Marketing and distribution expenses

- Legal/audit costs
- Other operating costs

The expense ratio is a percentage of the fund's AUM. The value of an expense ratio ***depends on the size of the fund.*** Different funds can have different expense ratios depending on the categories, debt, or equity.

- Expense Ratio is defined as the ratio of expenses incurred by a scheme to its Average Weekly Net Assets. This ratio should be as low as possible.

- Assume that a scheme has average weekly net assets of Rs 100 cr. and the scheme incurs Rs.1 cr. as annual expenses, then the expense ratio would be 1/ 100 = 1%.

- In case this scheme's expense ratio is comparable to or better than its peers then this scheme would qualify as a good investment, based on this parameter only.

- If this scheme performs well and its AUM increases to Rs. 150 cr in the next year whereas its annual expenses increase to Rs. 2 cr, then its expense would be 2/ 150 = 1.33%.

- It is not enough to compare a scheme's expense ratio with peers.

- The scheme's expense ratio must be tracked over different time periods.

- Ideally as net assets increase, the expense ratio of a scheme should come down.

What is portfolio turnover

The portfolio turnover ratio (PTR) ***is a percentage that indicates how often a mutual fund's assets are bought, sold, or changed over a one-year period.*** For example, ***if a fund's PTR is 25%, then 25% of its securities were bought or sold in the previous year.***

Generally, ***funds that are aggressively managed have higher PTRs than conservative funds.***

High PTRs can ***lead to increased fund management expenses and negative tax consequences.***

Funds with higher PTRs are more likely to incur capital gains taxes, which are then distributed to investors.

While churning increases the costs, it does not have any impact on the Expense Ratio, as transaction costs are not considered while calculating expense ratio.

Transaction costs are included in the buying & selling price of the scrip by way of brokerage, STT, cess, etc.

Portfolio Turnover is defined as *Lesser of Assets bought or sold/ Net Assets'*

- ABC Fund buys stocks worth Rs 800 crore and sells stocks worth Rs 900 crore over the last year

- The fund's average Assets Under Management (AUM) is Rs 1,600 crore

- The portfolio turnover is 800 crore / 1,600 crore x 100 (i.e. 50%)

A portfolio turnover ratio reflects the percentage of portfolio holdings that were changed, bought, or sold. A higher ratio has higher transaction costs, which can make fund management more expensive and impact fund returns. A lower ratio has lower transaction costs and makes fund management less expensive.

Here are some other examples of portfolio turnover ratios:

- A 5% portfolio turnover ratio suggests that 5% of the portfolio holdings changed over a one-year time period

- A ratio of 100% or greater indicates that all the securities in the fund were either sold or replaced with other holdings over a one-year period

- A fund with a 25% turnover rate holds stocks for four years on average

Generally, aggressively managed funds have higher portfolio turnover rates than do conservative funds which invest for the long term

How does AUM Affect Portfolio Turnover?

Assets under management (AUM) is a key metric for mutual funds. AUM can affect a mutual fund in several ways:

1) *Portfolio diversification*

A higher AUM can indicate that a fund's portfolio is more diversified.

2) *Income generation*

A higher AUM can indicate that a fund can generate more income from its investments.

3) _Liquidity_

A higher AUM can indicate that a fund is more liquid, making it easier for investors to buy and sell the fund.

4) _Expense ratio_

A higher AUM can indicate that a fund has higher costs. This is because mutual funds deduct a portion of returns to cover operational and administrative costs, known as the expense ratio. The expense ratio is unique to each fund and is influenced by its AUM size.

5) _Trust factor_

A higher AUM can indicate that a fund has a larger client base and a higher trust factor.

6) _Management experience_

A higher AUM can indicate that a fund house has better investment inflow, quality, and management experience.

AUM can vary over time depending on various factors such as market conditions, investor sentiment, and the performance of the fund.

In case the scheme _performs well and thereby attracts a lot of money flow, it may happen that the fund manager_ may not be able to deploy that extra money successfully as he may not find enough opportunities. Thus an increased fund size may result in lower returns.

✖ Exit Load

Exit Loads are paid by the investors in the scheme, if they exit one of the scheme before a specified time period. Exit Loads reduce the amount received by the investor. Not all schemes have an Exit Load, and not all schemes have similar exit loads as well.

> a) Mutual Fund exit load is a fee charged by the mutual fund houses if investors exit a scheme partially or fully within a certain period from the date of investment, as specified in the Scheme Information Document.
>
> b) Some schemes do not charge any exit fee. Mutual fund charges exit load to discourage investors from redeeming before a certain time period. This is done to protect the financial interest of all investors in the scheme, especially the ones who remain invested.

Different mutual funds _houses charge different fees for different schemes as an exit load._ If you want to invest for short tenures then you should understand the exit load structure of the scheme so that you can make informed investment decisions.

(Note:-Earlier there was a difference between the sale price and the NAV, the difference being the entry load'. However SEBI has banned entry loads since May 2009.)

Currently for equity funds / bonds funds redeemed within 1 year are charged 1% exit load. However liquid funds and money market funds normally have zero exit loads.

1) UTI mutual fund was set up in the Year _______________.

   a) **1963**

   b) 1986

   c) 1956

   d) 1947

2) Who establishes the Mutual Fund in India?

   a) **Securities Exchange Board of India**

   b) Asset Management Company

   c) Sponsor

   d) Shareholders

3) _______________ Mutual fund company was set up as a joint venture between RBI and Government of India

   a) **UTI MF**

   b) LIC MF

   c) SBI MF

   d) ICICI MF

4) In India, AMC must be registered with_____________.

   a) Company's Act, 2013

   b) No registration required.

   c) **Securities Exchange Board of India**

   d) Reserve Bank of India

5) ___________ is a type of investment vehicle consisting of a portfolio of stocks, bonds, or other securities.

a) Government Securities

b) **Mutual Funds**

c) Derivatives

d) Shares

6) The value of one unit of investment in Mutual fund is called the ___________.

a) **Net Asset Value**

b) Issue value

c) Market value

d) Gross Asset value

7) ___________ schemes not exposed to sudden and large movements of funds.

a) Fixed maturity plan

b) Open-Ended Funds

c) **Close-Ended Funds**

d) Interval fund

8) The feature of a mutual fund, where it spreads the investment in varied stocks and sectors by pooling the funds of various investors, is called as ___________.

a) Professional Management

b) Affordability

c) **Diversification**

d) Profit

9) Dividend income received from mutual in the hands of unit holders

a) Fully Taxable

b) **Fully Exempt**

c) Partly Exempt

d) Partly Taxable

10) Which of the following is not a limitation of mutual funds?

a) No guarantee of return

b) Fees and Expenses

c) Poor Performance

d) **Professional Management**

11) What are the reasons for economies of scale to the benefit of Mutual funds?

a) Large volumes of trade

b) **Portfolio diversification**

c) Risk reduction

d) Loss

12) High yield bonds have ______ potentials.

a) **High**

b) Low

c) Average

d) Nil

13) Tracking Error of _______ fund has to be minimised.

a) **Index funds**

b) Hybrid funds

c) Equity funds

d) Debt funds

14) Mutual funds are constituted in India as ____________.

a) **Trusts**

b) Limited liability partnership

c) Companies

d) Non-Government organisations

15) Investment in ___________ funds is best suited for investors with high-risk appetite and have good knowledge of the stock market.

a) Large-cap funds

b) Mid-cap funds

c) **Small-cap funds**

d) Multi-cap funds

16) Which amongst the following mutual fund schemes will generate higher returns?

a) Those investing in bonds of companies with poor credit rating

b) Those investing in risk-free government securities

c) Those investing in bonds of companies with a high rating

d) **Those who invest in debt funds**

17) Which amongst the following is an example of a physical asset?

a) Bank Deposit

b) Units by real estate investment trusts

c) Shares held in physical form

d) **Real estate**

18) A _________ fund invests in growth stocks (an emerging company) to attain maximum capital appreciation.

a) Debt funds

b) Gilt funds

c) **Growth funds**

d) Balanced funds

19) AMC look after administrative functions of a mutual fund for which they chrge _________

a) **Administrative fees**

b) Professional fees

c) Management fees

d) Processing fees

20) AMFI was incorporated on ________________.

a) **22nd August 1995**

b) 12th April 1992

c) 1st April 1935

d) 15th August 1947

21) Mutual Fund schemes are first offered to investors through.

a) Stock exchange

b) **New Fund Offer**

c) Initial Public Offer

d) AMFI

22) A Mutual fund is owned by _______________.

a) SEBI

b) The Government of India

c) AMFI

d) **All its investors**

23) The _________ can issue offer documents on behalf of the trustees

a) Custodian

b) **AMC**

c) Trustee

d) Sponsor

24) Expenses incurred that are above the regulatory limit are borne by sponsor & _____

a) AMC

b) Trustee

c) Sponsor

d) **All of the above**

25) A fund with _____ Sharpe ratio than the market is outperforming the market.

a) **Higher**

b) Lower

c) Average

d) Nil

26) _________ funds tends to have lower expense than other type of mutual funds

a) Equity funds

b) Debt Funds

c) Balance Funds

d) **Index funds**

27) Equity funds are exempt from long term capital gain tax when investments are held for at least ………… months from the date of acquisition

a) 6 months

b) **12 months**

c) 36 months

d) 9 months

28) Which of the following is not the characteristic of the mutual fund

a) Consistent investment process

b) Strong fund management

c) **Diversity in interest rate**

d) Difference from the benchmark

29) Which of the following is not the reason for the investment in mutual fund

a) professional management of the funds

b) Investment as low as 500 in any stock

c) **Personal customised portfolio**

d) Anytime buy or sell the instrument

30) A diversified equity fund is one which

a) Invests in one sector

b) Invests in one theme

c) **Invests in stocks across various sectors**

d) Invests in minimum 30 stocks

31) A mutual fund with a lower NAV or Net Asset Value is cheaper than one with a higher NAV?

a) **True**

b) False

32) Banks are regulated by Reserve Bank of India. Mutual funds are regulated by?

a) **Securities & Exchange Board of India**

b) Association of Mutual Funds In India (AMFI)

c) Reserve Bank of India

d) Ministry of Finance, Govt of India

33) Income scheme mutual funds invests primarily in __________?

a) **Fixed income securities**

b) Equities

c) Other Mutual Funds

d) Commercial Papers

34) Name the mutual fund scheme that provides tax benefits under 80C?

a) Gilt Funds

b) Fixed Income Fund

c) **Equity Linked Saving Scheme (ELSS)**

d) Growth Funds

35) What is the maximum period for which New Fund Offer (NFO) can remain open in) market?

a) 45 days

b) 30 days

c) **15 days**

d) 10 days

36) The NAV of mutual fund scheme calculated by mutual fund on ___basis

a) Yearly

b) Monthly

c) Weekly

d) **Daily**

37) Who conducts the certification that have to be passed by persons/ entities engaged in marketing and selling of mutual funds?

1. SEBI

2. AMFI

3. IRDAI

4. PFRDA

38) Fund of funds (FoF) mutual funds invests in __________

1. Equities

2. Corporate Bonds

3. G-Sec

4. **Other Mutual Funds**

39) A close-ended mutual fund has a fixed :

a) NAV

b) **fund size**

c) rate of return

d) number of distributor

40)   The maximum load that a fund can charge is determined by the :

a. AMC

b. **SEBI**

c. AMFI

d. distribution agents based on demand of all

41   The NAV of a mutual fund:

a) Is always constant

b) Keeps going up at a steady rate

c) **Fluctuates with market price movements**

d) cannot go down at all l

42)   An investor in a close-ended mutual fund can get his/her money back by selling his/her units:

a) back to the fund

b) To a special trust at NAV

c) **On stock exchange where fund is listed**

d) To the agent where he subscribe to the units of the fund

Define the following

1. Index fund
2. Equity fund
3. Arbitrage fund
4. Multi cap fund
5. Quant fund
6. ELSS
7. Funds of fund
8. SID
9. SAI
10. NAV

Short question

1. What are the different schemes offered by mutual fund
2. What is the role of AMC?

3. What is NFO?

4. What is the role of Registrar and transfer agent in mutual fund ?

5. What is the portfolio turnover?

6. What is the difference between entry and exit load

Short question

1. Who manages investors' money and How?

2. What is the difference between open and close ended funds

3. What is the tracking error

4. What are the diversified large cap funds

5. What is the growth scheme with example

6. What are the contents of Key information document

7. How does AUM effects portfolio Turnover

Long question

1. What is the Indian scenario with respect to mutual fund

2. What are the rights and duties of the investors in mutual fund scheme

3. What is the procedure of investing in NFO

4. There are the number of the scheme available in mutual fund, if investor wants to invest in any scheme that need to generate capital appreciation, which Scheme, he will choose and why?

5. There are basic documents available in mutual fund schemes to know in detail if an investor want to check the statutory information which document he will check and why?

6. If there are two mutual fund scheme namely ABC and XYZ.The ABC mutual fund scheme is having 1% expense ratio and XYZ company is having 2% expense ratio. According to you which scheme is good for the investor?

Unit 4
ETFs, Debt and Liquid Funds

Exchange Traded fund

Meaning

Exchange Traded Funds (ETFs) are mutual fund units which investors buy/ sell from the stock exchange, as against a normal mutual fund unit, where the investor buys / sells through a distributor or directly from the AMC.

ETF and How it Differ from Mutual fund

a) ETF as a concept is relatively new in India. **<u>It was only in early nineties that the concept gained in popularity in the USA.</u>**

b) ETFs have relatively lesser costs as compared to a mutual fund scheme. **This is largely due to the structure of ETFs.**

c) While in case of a mutual fund scheme, the AMC deals directly with the investors or distributors, the ETF structure is such that the AMC does not have to deal directly with investors or distributors. It instead issues units to a few designated large participants, who are also called as Authorised Participants (APs), who in turn act as market makers for the ETFs.

d) The Authorised Participants provide two way quotes for the ETFs on the stock exchange, which enables investors to buy and sell the ETFs at any given point of time when the stock markets are open for trading.

e) ETFs therefore trade like stocks. Buying and selling ETFs is similar to buying and selling shares on the stock exchange. Prices are available on real time and the ETFs can be purchased through a stock exchange broker just like one would buy / sell shares.

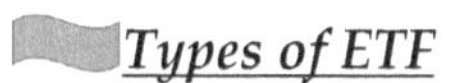 *Types of ETF*

1) Equity ETF

Equity ETFs are described as passive investment options combining the features of stocks and equity mutual funds. *Investors can trade these funds on stock exchanges, namely the NSE (National Stock Exchange) or BSE (Bombay Stock Exchange). They can purchase or sell these funds at market prices on a real-time basis.*

While the **minimum investment quantum is one unit,** there is no specification regarding the minimum investment amount. Equity ETFs are cost-effective and provide transparency regarding their holdings.

2) Bond ETF

Through bond ETFs, investors receive exposure to various *fixed-income instruments such as Government bonds (with different maturities) and debentures.* These ETFs combine the features of stock investments with the benefit of debt investments and the simplicity of mutual funds. People can trade bond ETFs or the open cash market.

3) Commodity ETF

Gold and silver ETFs are the only commodity ETFs available in India right now. These are passively managed funds tracking an underlying market index. *The NA (Net Asset Value) of commodity ETFs is subject to change throughout the day.* The movement in prices depends on the demand and supply of the commodity in the markets.

4) Sectoral/thematic ETF

A sectoral or thematic ETF tracks the performance of a particular sector or theme. *A sectoral Exchange Traded Fund invests in a specific industry, such as banking, pharmaceuticals, and real estate.* A thematic ETF focuses on an idea that encompasses multiple sectors like consumption or ESG (Environmental, Social, and Governance).

Salient features of ETF

1) *Hiring Broker*

An Exchange Traded Fund (ETF) is essentially a scheme where the investor has to buy/ sell units from the market through a broker

2) *Demat Account*

An investor must have a demat account for buying ETFs. You need a demat account to buy or sell Exchange Traded Funds (ETFs). You also need a trading account to hold funds and support transactions on the exchange

3) *Liquidity*

ETFs can be bought and sold on stock exchanges at any time of day, however, some funds are more popular than others. The easier it is to find a willing seller or buyer for a fund that is traded on a regular basis.

4) *Lower costs*

Compared to typical <u>mutual funds,</u> ETFs have substantially lower expense ratios. While a typical Index fund would have expenses in the range of 1.5% of Net Assets, an ETF might have expenses around 0.75%.

5) *Transparency*

Unlike mutual funds, which are only required to reveal their holdings every three months, ETFs are required to report their holdings and NAV on a daily basis for both open-ended and closed-ended schemes.

Buying and selling of ETF

a) An investor can approach a trading member of NSE and enter into an agreement with the trading member.

b) Buying and selling ETFs requires the investor to have demat and trading accounts. The procedure is exactly similar to buying and selling shares. The investor needs to have sufficient money in the trading account.

c) Once this is done, the investor needs to tell the broker precisely how many units he wants to buy/ sell and at what price.

d) Investors should take care that they place the order completely. They should not tell the broker to buy/ sell according to the broker's judgement.

e) Investors should also not keep signed delivery instruction slips with the broker as there may be a possibility of their misuse. Placing signed delivery instruction slips with the broker is similar to giving blank signed cheques to someone.

REITs (Real Estate Investment Trust)

REITs or Real Estate Investment Trusts are similar to mutual funds. They invest in real estate assets and give returns to the investor based on the return from the real estate. Like a mutual fund, REITs collect money from many investors and invest the same in real estate properties like offices, residential apartments, shopping malls, hotels, warehouses).

These REITs are listed on stock exchanges. The investors can directly buy and sell units from the stock exchanges.

Types :-

a) Equity REITs

Generate income by collecting rent on, and from sales of, the properties they own for the long-term.

b) Mortgage REITs

Also known as mREITs, invest in mortgages or mortgage securities tied to commercial and/or residential properties. Mortgage REITs don't own real estate, but finance real estate, instead. These REITs earn income from the interest on their investment

REITs offer regular income *in the form of dividends and capital appreciation.* They typically pay higher dividends than common equities and are able to generate higher yields due in part to the favourable tax structure.

Here are some other types of REITs:

- Office REITs: Own and operate office real estate and earn income by renting or leasing space to tenants in those properties.
- Diversified REITs: Own different types of properties

How Does a Company Qualify as a REIT?

To qualify as a REIT, a company has to meet specific requirements as mentioned below.

1. The entity needs to be structured as a business trust or a corporation.
2. Extends fully transferable shares.
3. Is managed by a team of trustees or a board of directors.
4. Must have a **minimum of 100 shareholders.**

5. Less than 5 individuals should not have held 50% of its share during each taxable year.

6. Is required **to pay at least 90% of the taxable income** as a dividend.

7. **Accrue a minimum 75% of gross income** from mortgage interest or rents.

8. A maximum of 20% of the corporation's assets comprises stock under taxable REIT subsidiaries.

9. **A minimum of 75% of investment assets** must be in real estate.

10. A minimum of 95% of REITs total income should be invested.

Gold ETF

Gold ETFs (G-ETFs) are a special type of ETF which invests in Gold and Gold related securities.

This product gives the investor an option to diversify his investments into a different asset class, other than equity and debt.

Traditionally, Indians are known to be big buyers of Gold; an age old tradition. Gold as an asset class is considered to be safe

This is because gold prices are difficult to manipulate and therefore enjoy better pricing transparency. When other financial markets are weak, gold gives good returns. It also enjoys the benefit of liquidity in case of any emergency.

Features of GOLD ETF

- **Reduced costs:** Gold ETFs are cost-effective because they eliminate storage costs and making charges, and have a low expense ratio.

- **Tax savings:** Investing in Gold ETFs can offer tax savings because GST credit is offset.

- **Reduced equity market fluctuations:** Investing in gold can lower fluctuations in equity markets.

- **Non-equity assets:** Gold ETFs are treated as non-equity assets, so their definition of short term is three years instead of one.

- **Pure gold:** SEBI regulations require Gold ETFs to buy gold that is at least 99.5 percent pure as per the LBMA standards

ADVANTAGES AND DISADVANTAGES OF PHYSICAL GOLD

Physical gold is a direct investment and it is actual gold that you can hold in your hand, such as coins, bars or jewellery. However, gold ETFs are an indirect investment because investors do not take ownership of gold itself. Instead, they buy shares of the ETF, which may hold gold, or it may use futures contracts to track the price of gold.

Benefits of Physical Gold

- Tangible asset: Physical gold is a tangible asset that you can see and touch, which some investors find more attractive than an intangible asset.

- No counterparty risk: With physical gold, you don't have to worry about counterparty risk, which is the risk that the person or company you are dealing with will default on their obligations.

- Potential for appreciation: Physical gold has the potential to appreciate in value over time, making it a good investment for those looking for long-term gains.

Risks of Physical Gold

- High transaction costs: When you buy physical gold, you'll likely have to pay a premium over the spot price, and when you sell, you may receive less than the spot price.

- Storage and security concerns: If you own physical gold, you'll need to find a safe place to store it, which can be costly and inconvenient.

- Low liquidity: If you need to sell your physical gold quickly, you may have difficulty finding a buyer, especially if the market is in a downturn.

ADVANTAGES AND DISADVANTAGES OF GOLD -ETF

Benefits of Gold ETFs

- Low transaction costs: When you buy and sell gold ETFs, you pay a commission to your broker, which is typically much lower than the transaction costs associated with physical gold.

- Liquidity: Gold ETFs are highly liquid, meaning you can buy and sell shares quickly and easily.

- Diversification: With gold ETFs, you can invest in an asset that tends to perform with low correlation to other assets, which can help spread risk in a portfolio.

Risks of Gold ETFs

- No tangible asset: Unlike physical gold, gold ETFs are not a tangible asset, which may make some investors uncomfortable during volatile market conditions.

- Counterparty risk: When you invest in a gold ETF, you are exposed to counterparty risk, meaning that if the ETF's issuer defaults, you could lose some or all of your investment.

- Tracking error: Gold ETFs may not track the price of gold perfectly, meaning investors may not get the full benefit of a rise in the price of gold.

(Note:-We buy Gold, among other things for children's marriages, for gifting during ceremonies etc. Holding physical Gold can have its' other disadvantages:

1. Fear of theft 2. Payment Wealth Tax 3. No surety of quality 4. Changes in fashion and trends 5. Locker costs 6. Lesser realisation on remoulding of ornaments)

Say for example 1 G-ETF = 1 gm of 99.5% pure Gold, then buying 1 G-ETF unit every month for 20 years would have given the investor a holding of 240gm of Gold, by the time his child's marriage approaches (240 gm = 1 gm/ month * 12 months * 20 Years). After 20 years the investor can convert the G-ETFs into 240 gm of physical gold by approaching the mutual fund or sell the G-ETFs in the market at the current price and buy 240 gms. of gold.

➡ *Working of Gold ETF*

A gold ETF is a type of investment fund that holds *gold assets, such as bullion or futures contracts, and is traded on a stock exchange.* The price of the ETF is directly linked to the price of gold, and investors can buy and sell shares of the ETF on the stock exchange just like they would with any other stock.

For example, if the price of gold increases by 1%, the value of the ETF should also increase by approximately 1%. Similarly, if the price of gold decreases, the value of the ETF should decrease as well.

When an investor buys shares of a gold ETF, they are essentially buying a portion of the gold held by the fund. This means that investors do not own physical gold, but instead own a share of the ETF that represents a certain amount of gold. For example, if an investor buys one share of a gold ETF that holds 10 ounces of gold, that investor effectively owns 1/10 of an ounce of gold.

a) The G-ETF is designed *as an open ended scheme*

b) Investors can *buy/ sell units any time at the prevailing market price.* This is an important point of differentiation of ETFs from similar open ended funds.

c) In case of open ended funds, *investors get units (or the units are redeemed) at a price based upon that day's NAV.*

d) In the case of ETFs, investors can buy (or sell) units at a price *which is prevailing that point of time during market hours.* Thus for all investors of open ended schemes, on any given day their buying (or redemption) price will be same, whereas for ETF investors, the prices will vary for each, depending upon when they bought (or sold) units on that day

⟹ *During New Fund Offer (NFO)*

* AMC decides of launching G-ETF

* The SID, SAI and KIM are prepared as per SEBI guidelines Investors invest in the fund and the AMC gives units to investors in return AMC buys Gold of specified quality at the prevailing rates

⟹ *On an ongoing basis*

Authorised Participants (typically large institutional investors) give money/ Gold to AMC

AMC gives equivalent number of units bundled together to these authorised participants (AP)

APs split these bundled units into individual units and offer for sale in the secondary market

Investors can buy G-ETF units from the secondary markets either from the quantity being sold by the APs or by other retail investors

Retail investors can also sell their units in the market

The Gold which the AP deposits for buying the bundled ETF units is known as _*Portfolio Deposit'.*

This Portfolio Deposit has to be deposited with the Custodian. A custodian is someone who handles the physical Gold for the AMC.

The AMC signs an agreement with the Custodian, where all the terms and conditions are agreed upon.

Once the AP deposits Gold with the custodian, it is the responsibility of the custodian to ensure safety of the Gold, otherwise he has to bear the liability, to the extent of the market value of the Gold.

The custodian has to keep record of all the Gold that has been deposited/ withdrawn under the G-ETF. An account is maintained for this purpose, which is known as _Allocated Account'.

The custodian, on a daily basis, enters the inflows and outflows of Gold bars from this account. All details such as the serial number, refiner, fineness etc. are maintained in this account. The transfer of Gold from or into the Allocated Account happens at the end of each business day.

A report is submitted by the custodian, no later than the following business day, to the AMC.

The money which the AP deposits for buying the bundled _**ETF units is known as 'Cash Component'.**_

This Cash Component is paid to the AMC. The Cash Component is not mandatory and is paid to adjust for the difference between the applicable NAV and the market value of the Portfolio Deposit.

This difference may be due to accrued dividend, management fees, etc. _The bundled units (which the AP receives on payment of Portfolio Deposit to the custodian and Cash Component to the AMC)_ **are known as Creation Units.**

Each Creation Unit comprises of a predefined number of ETFs Units (say 25,000 or 100 or any other number). Thus, now it can be said that Authorised Participants pay Portfolio Deposit and/ or Cash Component and get Creation Units in return. Each Creation Unit consists of a pre-defined number of G-ETF Units. APs strip these Creation Units (which are nothing but bundled G-ETF units) and sell individual G-ETF units in the market. Thus retail investors can buy/ sell 1 unit or it's multiples in the secondary market

Sovereign Gold Bonds

➤ 1) _**What is Sovereign Gold Bond (SGB)? Who is the issuer?**_

SGBs are government securities denominated in grams of gold. They are substitutes for holding physical gold. Investors have to pay the issue price in cash and the bonds will be redeemed in cash on maturity. The Bond is issued by the Reserve Bank on behalf of the Government of India.

➤ 2) _**Why should I buy SGB rather than physical gold? What are the benefits?**_

The quantity of gold for which the investor pays is protected, since he receives the ongoing market price at the time of redemption/ premature redemption. The SGB offers a superior alternative to holding gold in physical form. The risks and costs of storage are eliminated. Investors are assured of the market value of gold at the time of maturity and periodical interest. SGB is free from issues like making charges and purity in the case of gold in jewellery form. The bonds are held in the books of the RBI or in demat form eliminating risk of loss of scrip etc.

➤ 3) **Are there any risks in investing in SGBs?**

There may be a risk of capital loss if the market price of gold declines. However, the investor does not lose in terms of the units of gold which he has paid for.

➡ **4) Who is eligible to invest in the SGBs?**

Persons resident in India as defined under Foreign Exchange Management Act, 1999 are eligible to invest in SGB. Eligible investors include individuals, HUFs, trusts, universities and charitable institutions. Individual investors with subsequent change in residential status from resident to non-resident may continue to hold SGB till early redemption/maturity.

➡ **5) Whether joint holding will be allowed?**

Yes, joint holding is allowed.

➡ **6) I Can a Minor invest in SGB?**

Yes. The application on behalf of the minor has to be made by his/her guardian.

➡ **7) Where can investors get the application form?**

The application form will be provided by the issuing banks/SHCIL offices/ designated Post Offices/agents. It can also be downloaded from the RBI's website. Banks may also provide online application facilities.

➡ **8) What are the Know-Your-Customer (KYC) norms?**

Every application must be accompanied by the 'PAN Number' issued by the Income Tax Department to the investor(s).

9) Can an investor hold more than one investor ID for subscribing to the Sovereign Gold Bond?

No. An investor can have only one unique investor Id linked to any of the prescribed identification documents. The unique investor ID is to be used for all the subsequent investments in the scheme. For holding securities in dematerialized form, quoting of PAN in the application form is mandatory.

10) What is the minimum and maximum limit for investment?

The Bonds are issued in denominations of one gram of gold and in multiples thereof. Minimum investment in the Bond shall be one gram with a maximum limit of subscription of 4 kg for individuals, 4 kg for Hindu Undivided Family (HUF) and 20 kg for trusts and similar entities notified by the government from time to time per fiscal year (April – March). In case of joint holding, the limit applies to the first applicant. The annual ceiling will include bonds subscribed under different tranches during initial issuance by Government and those purchased from the secondary market. The ceiling on investment will not include the holdings as collateral by banks and other Financial Institutions

11) Can each member of my family buy 4Kg in their own name?

Yes, each family member can buy the bonds in his/her own name if they satisfy the eligibility criteria as defined at Q No.4.

12) Can an investor/trust buy 4 Kg/20 Kg worth of SGB every year?

Yes. An investor/trust can buy 4 Kg/20 Kg worth of gold every year as the ceiling has been fixed on a fiscal year (April-March) basis.

13) *Is the maximum limit of 4 Kg applicable in case of joint holding?*

The maximum limit will be applicable to the first applicant in case of a joint holding for that specific application.

14) *What is the rate of interest and how will the interest be paid?*

The Bonds bear interest at the rate of 2.50 per cent (fixed rate) per annum on the amount of initial investment. Interest will be credited semi-annually to the bank account of the investor and the last interest wille be payable on maturity along with the principal.

15) *Who are the authorised agencies selling the SGBs?*

Bonds are sold through offices or branches of Nationalised Banks, Scheduled Private Banks, Scheduled Foreign Banks, designated Post Offices, Stock Holding Corporation of India Ltd. (SHCIL) and the authorised stock exchanges either directly or through their agents.

16) *If I apply, am I assured of allotment?*

If the customer meets the eligibility criteria, produces a valid identification document and remits the application money on time, he/she will receive the allotment.

17) *When will the customers be issued Holding Certificate?*

The customers will be issued Certificate of Holding on the date of issuance of the SGB. Certificate of Holding can be collected from the issuing banks/SHCIL offices/Post Offices/Designated stock exchanges/agents or obtained directly from RBI on email, if email address is provided in the application form.

18) *Can I apply online?*

Yes. A customer can apply online through the website of the listed scheduled commercial banks. The issue price of the Gold Bonds will be ₹ 50 per gram less than the nominal value to those investors applying online and the payment against the application is made through digital mode.

19) *At what price the bonds are sold?*

Thec nominal value of Gold Bonds shall be in Indian Rupees fixed on the basis of simple average of closing price of gold of 999 purity, published by the India Bullion and Jewelers Association Limited, for the last 3 business days of the week preceding the subscription period.

20) *Will RBI publish the rate of gold applicable every day?*

The price of gold for the relevant tranche will be published on RBI website two days before the issue opens.

21) *What will I get on redemption?*

On maturity, the Gold Bonds shall be redeemed in Indian Rupees and the redemption price shall be based on the simple average of closing price of gold of 999 purity of previous 3 business days from the date of repayment, published by the India Bullion and Jewelers Association Limited.

22) *How will I get the redemption amount?*

Both interest and redemption proceeds will be credited to the bank account furnished by the customer at the time of buying the bond.

23) *What are the procedures involved during redemption?*

- *The investor will be advised one month before maturity regarding the ensuing maturity of the bond.*
- *On the date of maturity, the maturity proceeds will be credited to the bank account as per the details on record.*
- *In case there are changes in any details, such as, account number, email ids, then the investor must intimate the bank/SHCIL/PO promptly.*

24) *Can I encash the bond anytime I want? Is premature redemption allowed?*

Though the tenor of the bond is 8 years, early encashment/redemption of the bond is allowed after fifth year from the date of issue on coupon payment dates. The bond will be tradable on Exchanges, if held in demat form. It can also be transferred to any other eligible investor.

25) *What do I have to do if I want to exit my investment?*

In case of premature redemption, investors can approach the concerned bank/ SHCIL offices/Post Office/agent thirty days before the coupon payment date. Request for premature redemption can only be entertained if the investor approaches the concerned bank/post office at least one more day before the coupon payment date. The proceeds will be credited to the customer's bank account provided at the time of applying for the bond.

26) *Can I gift the bonds to a relative or friend on some occasion?*

The bond can be gifted/transferable to a relative/friend/anybody who fulfills the eligibility criteria (as mentioned at Q.no. 4). The Bonds shall be transferable in accordance with the provisions of the Government Securities Act 2006 and the Government Securities Regulations 2007 before maturity by execution of an instrument of transfer which is available with the issuing agents.

27) *Can I use these securities as collateral for loans?*

Yes, these securities are eligible to be used as collateral for loans from banks, financial Institutions and Non-Banking Financial Companies (NBFC). The Loan to Value ratio will be the same as applicable to ordinary gold loans prescribed by RBI from time to time. Granting loan against SGBs would be subject to the decision of the bank/financing agency, and cannot be inferred as a matter of right.

28) *What are the tax implications on i) interest and ii) capital gain?*

Interest on the Bonds will be taxable as per the provisions of the Income-tax Act, 1961 (43 of 1961). The capital gains tax arising on redemption of SGB to an individual has been exempted. The indexation benefits will be provided to long term capital gains arising to any person on transfer of bond.

29) *Is tax deducted at source (TDS) applicable on the bond?*

TDS is not applicable on the bond. However, it is the responsibility of the bond holder to comply with the tax laws.

30) *Who will provide other customer services to the investors after issuance of the bonds?*

The issuing banks/SHCIL offices/Post Offices/Designated stock exchanges/ agents through which these securities have been purchased will provide other customer services such as change of address, early redemption, nomination, grievance redressal, transfer applications etc.

31) *What are the payment options for investing in the Sovereign Gold Bonds?*

Payment can be made through cash (upto ₹ 20000)/cheques/demand draft/ electronic fund transfer.

32) *Whether nomination facility is available for these investments?*

Yes, nomination facility is available as per the provisions of the Government Securities Act 2006 and Government Securities Regulations, 2007. A nomination form is available along with Application form. An individual Non - resident Indian may get the security transferred in his name on account of his being a nominee of a deceased investor provided that:

- *the Non-Resident investor shall need to hold the security till early redemption or till maturity; and*

- *the interest and maturity proceeds of the investment shall not be repatriable.*

33) *Can I get the bonds in demat form?*

Yes. The bonds can be held in demat account. A specific request for the same must be made in the application form itself.

Till the process of dematerialization is completed, the bonds will be held in RBI's books. The facility for conversion to demat will also be available subsequent to allotment of the bond.

34) . *Can I trade these bonds?*

The bonds are tradable from a date to be notified by RBI. (It may be noted that only bonds held in demat form with depositories can be traded in stock exchanges) The bonds can also be sold and transferred as per provisions of Government Securities Act, 2006. Partial transfer of bonds is also possible.

MARKET MAKING BY APS

APs are like market makers and continuously offer two way quotes (buy and sell). They earn on the difference between the two way quotes they offer. This difference is known as bid-ask spread. They provide liquidity to the ETFs by continuously offering to buy and sell ETF units.

For Example:-If the last traded price of a G-ETF is Rs 1000, then an AP will give a two way quote by offering to buy an ETF unit at Rs 999 and offering to sell an ETF unit Rs. 1001. Thus whenever the AP buys, he will buy @ 999 and when he sells, he will sell at 1001, thereby earning Rs. 2 as the difference. It should also be understood that the impact of this transaction is that the AP does not increase/ decrease his holding in the ETF.

This is known as earning through Dealer Spreads. APs also play an important role of aligning the price of the unit with the NAV. This is done by exploiting the arbitrage opportunities.

APs and market makers both play pivotal roles in ensuring that ETF trading is smooth, in all market conditions. A market maker is essentially a broker-dealer that provides two-sided (buy and sell) quotes to clients regularly. Market makers are key liquidity providers in the ETF ecosystem.

An AP is a financial institution, often a bank, that dynamically manages the creation and redemption of ETF shares in the primary market. This process adjusts the number of ETF shares outstanding and helps keep an ETF's price aligned with the value of its underlying securities.

Features

1) *Manage the supply of ETF shares*

APs are the only investors allowed to interact directly with the fund. They can change the supply of ETF shares on the market to help keep an ETF's price aligned with the value of its underlying securities.

2) *Profit from premiums*

For example, if the value of the underlying securities falls to falls while the price of ETF remain same, AP will earn profit by creating new ETF

3) *Provide liquidity*

APs provide a large portion of the liquidity in the ETF market by obtaining the underlying assets required to create the shares of an ETF.

An authorised participant is an organisation that has the right to create and redeem shares of an exchange traded fund (ETF). They provide a large portion of the liquidity in the ETF market by obtaining the underlying assets required to create the shares of an ETF.

➤ *Role of Custodian in Gold -ETF*

a) As explained earlier, *the custodian maintains record of all the Gold that comes into and goes out of the scheme's Portfolio Deposit.*

b) The custodian makes *respective entries in the Allocated Account* thus transferring Gold into and out of the scheme at the end of each business day.

c) The custodian has *no right on the Gold in the Allocated Account.* The custodian may appoint a sub-custodian to perform some of the duties. The custodian *charges fee for the services rendered* and has to *buy adequate insurance for the Gold held.* The premium paid for the insurance is borne by the scheme as a transaction cost and is allowed as an expense under SEBI guidelines. This expense contributes in a small way to the tracking error.

d) *The difference between the returns given by Gold and those delivered by the scheme is known as Tracking Error.* It is defined as the variance between the daily returns of the underlying (Gold in this case) and the NAV of the scheme for any given time period. Gold has to be valued as per a specific formula mandated by regulations.

Creation units, Portfolio Deposit and Cash Component (an example):

Let us look at the following example to understand Creation Units, Portfolio Deposit and Cash Component in detail.

1. Assumption: 1 ETF unit = 1 gm of 99.5% pure Gold During New Fund Offer (NFO) Amount Invested (Rs.): 5000 Price of 1 gm of Gold (Rs.): 1000

2. Since 1 ETF unit = 1 gm of Gold Issue Price (Rs.) = 1000

3. Units Allotted (Number = Investment/ Issue Price): 5

➡️ _Creation unit:_ The minimum number of ETF shares required to transact directly with the ETF issuer. Primary market: The direct exchange of securities for shares of an ETF between authorised participants and ETF issuers.

- **Creation Units 1 Creation Unit = 100 ETF units**

- **NAV (Rs.) = 1050 Price of 1 gm of Gold (Rs.): 1000**

- **So, 100 Units will cost (Rs.) = 1050 * 100 = 1,05,000**

- **100 ETF will be equal to 100 gm of Gold**

- **Therefore, value of Portfolio Deposit (Rs.) = 1000 * 100 = 1,00,000**

- **Hence Cash Component (Rs.) = 1,05,000 – 1,00,000 = 5,000**

A cash component is a collateral margin that is created when securities are pledged. In an exchange-traded fund (ETF), the cash component is a portion of the conversion shares offer consideration that consists of cash.

A cash component is the difference between the net asset value (NAV) of a creation unit and the market value of a portfolio deposit. The cash component includes accrued dividends, annual charges, and residual cash

The cash component is an amount equal to the difference between the NAV of the fund shares and the deposit amount. The deposit amount is equal to the market value of the deposit securities.

Salient features of Debt fund

1. Debt funds are very liquid and _can be redeemed easily,_ usually within one or two working days of placing the redemption request.

2. Debt funds are funds which **invest money in debt instruments such as short and long term bonds, government securities, t-bills, corporate paper, commercial paper, call money etc.**

3. The main **investing objective of a debt fund is usually preservation of capital and generation of income. Thank**

4. **Debt funds pose low risk. The interest amount is fixed. The principal you invest is returned to you at a fixed time as well.**

5. Debt _markets in India are wholesale in nature and hence retail investors generally find it difficult to directly participate in the debt markets._

6. Not many **understand the relationship between interest rates and bond prices or the difference between Coupon and Yield.**

7. Debt funds **are comparatively less risk and stable over the other money market instruments as they are not dependent upon the market**

➤ _Coupon rate and yield to maturity_

A coupon rate is the annual interest rate paid on a bond by the issuer. It's calculated based on the bond's face value, not its market value or issue price.

Coupon rates are fixed and remain the same throughout the life of the bond. However, market interest rates can fluctuate, which can impact the bond's market price

For example, if you have a 10-year- Rs 2,000 bond with a coupon rate of 10 per cent, you will get Rs 200 every year for 10 years, no matter what happens to the bond price in the market.

➤ _Face value_

The face value of a bond is the amount that the issuer promises to pay to the bondholder when the bond reaches maturity. It's also known as the par value or redemption value. The face value is fixed when the bond is issued and is printed on the bond itself.

(For example, if a bond has a face value of $1,000, the bond will mature and be redeemed at this amount.)

A Ltd. has borrowed against a debt instrument, the rate be G-Sec plus 3%. Therefore if the GSec moves up, the rate of interest moves up and if the G-Sec moves down the interest rate moves down. Prima facie debt instruments looks risk free. However two important questions need to be asked here:

1) What if interest rates rise during the tenure of the loan?

2) What if the borrower fails to pay the interest and/ or fails to repay the principal?

➤ **Interest rate Risk**

Interest rate risk is the danger that the value of a bond or other fixed-income investment will suffer as the result of a change in interest rates.

How to reduce interest rate risk

- *Diversify:* Spread your investments across a range of assets and liabilities with different interest rate sensitivities.

- *Invest in safer options:* Invest in bonds and certificates with short maturity tenure. Securities with short maturity tenure are less likely to be affected by interest rate fluctuations.

- *Use hedging strategies:* Use financial instruments to offset the risk of interest rate changes. Common hedging strategies include interest rate swaps, options, and futures contracts.

- *Buy floating-rate bonds:* Floating-rate bonds pay variable interest rates throughout their tenure, which are usually tied to market fluctuations. When interest rates rise, the rate of return increases.

- *Adjust asset allocation:* Adjust the asset allocation of your investment.

Credit Rate Risk

Credit risk is the likelihood that a lender will lose money if they extend credit to a borrower. Credit risk can arise from the potential that a borrower will not perform on an obligation, such as failing to repay a loan.

Credit risk can impact a lender in several ways, including:

- Loss of principal and interest: A lender may not receive the principal and interest owed to them.

- Interrupted cash flows: A lender may experience an interruption of cash flows.

- Increased collection costs: A lender may face increased costs for collection.

This risk can be taken care of by investing in paper issued by companies with very high Credit Rating. The probability of a borrower with very high Credit Rating defaulting is far lesser than that of a borrower with low credit rating. Government paper is highest in safety when it comes to credit risk

Credit rating agencies assess the creditworthiness of a company and the risk factor associated with it. This helps banks and money lending companies make better investment decisions.

Here are some credit rating agencies in India:

- Credit Rating Information Services of India Limited (CRISIL)

- Investment Information and Credit Rating Agency of India Limited (ICRA)

- Credit Analysis & Research (CARE)

- Onida Individual Credit Rating Agency of India (ONICRA)

➡️ *Some of CRISIL's rating symbols are given below:*

CRISIL AAA	Securities with this rating are considered to have the highest degree of safety regarding timely servicing of financial obligations. Such securities carry lowest credit risk.
CRISIL AA	Securities with this rating are considered to have high degree of safety regarding timely servicing of financial obligations. Such securities carry very low credit risk.
CRISIL A	Securities with this rating are considered to have adequate degree of safety regarding timely servicing of financial obligations. Such securities carry low credit risk.
CRISIL BBB	Securities with this rating are considered to have moderate degree of safety regarding timely servicing of financial obligations. Such securities carry moderate credit risk.
CRISIL BB	Securities with this rating are considered to have moderate risk of default regarding timely servicing of financial obligations.
CRISIL B	Securities with this rating are considered to have high risk of default regarding timely servicing of financial obligations.
CRISIL C	Securities with this rating are considered to have very high risk of default regarding timely servicing of financial obligations.
CRISIL D	Securities with this rating are in default or are expected to be in default soon.

a) The price of an instrument (equity / bond) **is nothing but the present value of the future cash flows.**

b) In case of bonds, **there is no ambiguity about future cash flows,** as is the case of equities. Future cash flows in case of bonds are the periodic coupon payments that the investor will receive.

c) Future cash flows for equities are the dividends than the investor may receive. Bond coupon payments are known right at the beginning, whereas there is no surety about a share paying dividends to an investor.

d) Thus different investors/ analysts have different earning projections for equities, and hence each participant has a different view on the present value of a share. Bond cash flows being known, there is no confusion about what the present value of each future cash flow should be.

Compounding and discounting formulas

Compounding is the method that will be used to calculate the interest earned for investment invested for N number of years along with the principal amount

Suppose an investor invests Rs.100 (initial investment) in a bank FD @ 8% for 10 years, then to calculate the amount that he will receive after 10 years,

we will use the compound interest formula given below –

A = P * (1 + r)t

Substituting P = 100, r = 8% and t = 10 years,

A=100(1+8/100)^10

A=100(1+0.08)^10

A=100(1.08)^10

A=100(2.15892)

A=215.89

we get the value for A as Rs. 215.89.

This process is known as compounding.

Discounting Formula: Instead of calculating the final amount after 10 years, if the investor says he needs Rs.215.89 after 10 years and we know that a bank FD is offering 8% per annum,

We need to calculate how much money he should invest today to reach a value of Rs. 215.89 after 10 years.

Again we use the same formula, but slightly tweaked. Here we solve for P (initial investment), as against A in the previous example.

Discounting Formula

P = A / (1 + r)t

Substituting A = 215.89, r = 8% and t = 10 years,

we can find out the value of 100

Lets see

P=215.89/(1.08)^10

P=215.89/2.15892

P=100 (This process is the exact opposite of compounding and this is known as discounting.)

⟹ *Yield to maturity*

YTM is calculated by assuming that the bond buyer will hold it until its maturity date and reinvest each interest payment at the same interest rate. It's also the discount rate at which the sum of all future cash flows (from coupons and principal repayment) equals the price of the bond.

An important factor in bond pricing is the Yield to Maturity (YTM). This is rate applied to the future cash flow (coupon payment) to arrive at its present value. If the YTM increases, the present value of the cash flows will go down.

The cash flows for the bond and the Present Values (PVs) of these cash flows are as given below

8% Discounting	Year 0	Year 1	Year 2	Year 3
	Pay 100			
Present value of Rs.8 will be **P=8/(1.08)^1** **P=8/1.259712** **Present value will be =7.407**		First Year receive 8 rupees		
Present value of Rs.8 will be **P=8/(1.08)^2** **P=8/1.1664** **Present value will be =6.85**			Second year Interest Rs. 8	

Present value of Rs.8 will be P=108/(1.08)^3 P=108/1.259 Present value will be = 85.78 Note (at the end they are getting the principal amount with last year interest				Receive Rs. 108

Price = 7.41 + 6.86 + 85.73 = 100 (This is the Present Value of all the future cash flows in Year 1, Year 2 and Year 3)

Problems on compound interest

Find the compound interest (CI) on Rs. 12,600 for 2 years at 10% per annum compounded annually.

Solution:

Given,

Principal (P) = Rs. 12,600

Rate (R) = 10

Number of years (n) = 2

$A = P[1 + (R/100)]^n$

$= 12600[1 + (10/100)]^2$

$= 12600[1 + (1/10)]^2$

$= 12600 [(10 + 1)/10]^2$

$= 12600 \times (11/10) \times (11/10)$

$= 126 \times 121$

$= 15246$

A TV was bought for Rs. 21,000. The value of the TV was depreciated by 5% per annum. Find the value of the TV after 3 years. (Depreciation means the reduction of value due to use and age of the item)

Solution:

Principal (P) = Rs. 21,000

Rate of depreciation (R) = 5%

n = 3

Using the formula of CI for depreciation,

$A = P[1 - (R/100)]n$

$A = $ Rs. $21,000[1 - (5/100)]^3$

$= $ Rs. $21,000[1 - (1/20)]^3$

$= $ Rs. $21,000[(20 - 1)/20]^3$

$= $ Rs. $21,000 \times (19/20) \times (19/20) \times (19/20)$

$= $ Rs. $18,004.875$

Find the compound interest on Rs 48,000 for one year at 8% per annum when compounded half-yearly.

Solution:

Given,

Principal (P) = Rs 48,000

Rate (R) = 8% p.a.

Time (n) = 1 year

Also, the interest is compounded half-yearly.

So, $A = P[1 + (R/200)]^{2n}$

$= $ Rs. $48000[1 + (8/200)]^{2(1)}$

$= $ Rs. $48000[1 + (1/25)]^2$

$= $ Rs. $48000[(25 + 1)/25]^2$

$= $ Rs. $48,000 \times (26/25) \times (26/25)$

$= $ Rs. $76.8 \times 26 \times 26$

$= $ Rs $51,916.80$

Therefore, the compound interest = $A - P$

$= $ Rs $(519,16.80 - 48,000)$

$= $ Rs $3,916.80$

5. Find the compound interest on Rs. 8000 at 15% per annum for 2 years 4 months, compounded annually.

Solution:

Given,

Principal (P) = Rs. 8000

Rate of interest (R) = 15% p.a

Time (n) = 2 years 4 months

4 months = 4/12 years = 1/3 years

So,

A = P[1 + (R/100)]^n

= Rs. 8000 [1 + (15/100)]^2 [1 + (1/3) × (15/100)]

= Rs. 8000 [1 + (3/20)]^2 [1 + (3/20 × 3)]

= Rs. 8000 [(20 + 3)/20]^2 [(20 + 1)/20]

= Rs. 8000 × (23/20) × (23/20) × (21/20)

= Rs. 11,109

Therefore, the compound interest = A − P = Rs. 11,109 − Rs. 8000 = Rs. 3109

Find the compound interest on Rs 48,000 for one year at 8% per annum when compounded half-yearly.

Solution:

Given,

Principal (P) = Rs 48,000

Rate (R) = 8% p.a.

Time (n) = 1 year

Also, the interest is compounded half-yearly.

So, A = P[1 + (R/200)]^{2n}

= Rs. 48000[1 + (8/200)]$^{2(1)}$

= Rs. 48000[1 + (1/25)]^2

= Rs. 48000[(25 + 1)/25]^2

= Rs. 48,000 × (26/25) × (26/25)

= Rs. 76.8 × 26 × 26

= Rs 51,916.80

Therefore, the compound interest = A − P

= Rs (519,16.80 − 48,000)

= Rs 3,916.80

Find the compound interest on Rs. 8000 at 15% per annum for 2 years 4 months, compounded annually.

Solution:

Given,

Principal (P) = Rs. 8000

Rate of interest (R) = 15% p.a

Time (n) = 2 years 4 months

4 months = 4/12 years = 1/3 years

So,

$A = P[1 + (R/100)]^n$

$= \text{Rs. } 8000 \, [1 + (15/100)]^2 \, [1 + (1/3) \times (15/100)]$

$= \text{Rs. } 8000 \, [1 + (3/20)]^2 \, [1 + (3/20 \times 3)]$

$= \text{Rs. } 8000 \, [(20 + 3)/20]^2 \, [(20 + 1)/20]$

$= \text{Rs. } 8000 \times (23/20) \times (23/20) \times (21/20)$

$= \text{Rs. } 11{,}109$

Therefore, the compound interest = A – P = Rs. 11,109 – Rs. 8000 = Rs. 3109

Problem on Discounting method

Let us take the example of John who is expected to receive 1,000 after 4 years. Determine the present value of the sum today if the discount rate is 5%.

$P = A/[1 + (R/100)]^n$

$P = 1000/[1 + (5/100)]^4$

$P = 1000/[1 + (0.005)]^4$

$P = 1000/(1.005)^4$

$P = 1000/$1.02015

$P = $**980.24**

Let us take another example of a project having a life of 5 years with the following cash flow. Determine the present value of all the cash flows if the relevant discount rate is 6%.

$P = A/[1 + (R/100)]^n$

$P = 1000/[1 + (6/100)]^5$

$P = 1000/[1 + (0.006)]^5$

$P = 1000/(1.006)^5$

P=1000/1.0303

P=**970.87**

Fixed Maturity Plan (FMP)

A fixed maturity plan is a close-ended debt fund that comes with a fixed lock-in period and limited investment window. Individuals can only invest in such securities during new fund offers or NFO made by any asset management company through subscription requests.

Such corpus mainly consists of debt securities such as certificates of deposit, treasury bills, corporate bonds, etc.

FMPs are essentially close-ended debt schemes. The money received by the scheme is used by the fund managers to buy debt securities with maturities coinciding with the maturity of the scheme.

There is no rule which stops the fund manager from selling these securities earlier, but typically fund managers avoid it and hold on to the debt papers till maturity. Investors must look at the portfolio of FMPs before investing. If an FMP is giving a relatively higher _indicative yield', it may be investing in slightly riskier securities.

Thus investors must assess the risk level of the portfolio by looking at the credit ratings of the securities.

Characteristics of Fixed Maturity Plans

A fixed maturity plan has the following features-

• Lock-in period

Fixed maturity plans come with a stipulated lock-in period during which funds cannot be withdrawn from the scheme. The primary purpose of such stringent withdrawal rules is to ensure the deposit remains locked-in for a given tenure so that maximum returns can be generated from the underlying securities.

• Portfolio

Fixed maturity plan returns are generated through investment in debt tools such as government and corporate bonds, non-convertible debentures, treasury bills, certificates of deposit, commercial papers, securitised debt instruments, etc.

Such a portfolio is created by respective fund managers to ensure minimal risk is associated with total corpus, as stock market fluctuations have a relatively lower impact on such debt securities.

• Close-ended schemes

Individuals willing to invest in close-ended fixed maturity schemes can do so by subscribing to a new fund offer when announced by asset management companies. Only a limited number of **NAV** units are issued against such funds, which are traded in the share market like standard shares.

As a **fixed deposit** plan comes with a predetermined lock-in period, NAV units of such mutual funds can only be obtained during times of new fund offers.

• Quality assets

Portfolio managers primarily choose debt instruments issued by renowned companies to build a corpus that generates the highest fixed maturity plan returns. This reduces the risk factor associated with tools further, making it one of the **safest stock** market tools available.

Advantages of Fixed Maturity Plans

Investing in a fixed maturity plan comes with the following associated benefits –

• Lower risk

A fixed maturity plan is one of the most secure forms of investment as it primarily targets debt securities of renowned listed companies operating in a country. Debt tools act as a liability for a company, and thereby, are repaid first from annual revenues.

Also, such fixed maturity mutual funds come with high credit ratings as computed by the top credit rating agencies in the country, hence certifying the credibility of the scheme.

• Stability

Debt tools are subject to relatively lower fluctuations arising from stock market fluctuations. Also, during times of recession in a country, the bonds become more profitable as investors shift towards less risky instruments, allowing individuals to enjoy high returns from their investment.

Limitations of a Fixed Maturity Plan

a) Relatively lower yields

Fixed maturity returns are comparatively lower than corresponding investments in equity funds, as the return percentage remains fixed throughout the tenure of investment. Consequently, investors fail to benefit from any positive cyclical movement of the stock market, as interest incomes remain constant for such schemes.

b) Stringent lock-in period

Investing in a fixed maturity plan implies that the principal amount has to be kept locked in for a stipulated period, without the benefit of partial withdrawals. This might pose a burden on the liquidity requirements of investors.

Capital protection Fund

A capital protection fund is a closed-end hybrid mutual fund that aims to protect investors' capital during market downturns.

It does this by investing in fixed income options and equity, and by providing a return in parallel with the participation ratio of the investors.

The allocation between equity and debt is usually based on the bond yield and the term of the scheme. The fund's investment in debt securities is exposed to default risk, which means there is a risk that payments on these securities will not be made.

Advantages of investing in CPOS (capital protection oriented scheme) funds

Here are some of the major advantages of investing in a CPOS fund for an investor.

a) The capital protection funds are extremely suited to investors who are generally spooked by the volatility in stock markets.

b) CPOs ensure that the capital is protected but at the same time, the much needed alpha is provided by the equity component in the portfolio.

c) Being closed ended, the CPOS normally do not have to worry about redemption pressures and can take a longer term view of capital protection.

d) The investor gets the best of both worlds as they earn stable returns from the 80% allocation to debt while the equity component ensures alpha.

e) If equity markets are on a rise in three to five years you could see your investments grow well.

f) However, even if the equity markets see negative returns, capital is still protected and that is a big consolation to the investor.

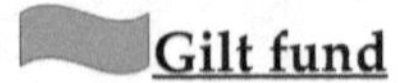# Gilt fund

Gilt funds are one of the oldest investment options in India; these existed even during the pre- independence period. _Essentially, gilt funds invest your money in debt securities issued by the government._ As securities offered by the government are known to be a safe investment avenue, gilt funds are an excellent choice for risk-averse investors.

The debt securities generate interest income through which the gilt fund investors earn their returns. The performance of any gilt fund depends on how the interest rate moves. Hence, gilt funds are highly recommended during the falling rate regime. It is because as the interest rates fall, prices start rising. This leads to an increase in the Net Assest Value (NAV) of gilt funds. Due to this reason, a lot of investors switch to gilt funds when the interest rates start falling.

Benefits of Investing in Gilt Funds

a) Zero Credit Risk

Unlike mutual funds that invest in corporate bonds where there is always significant credit risk, gilt funds have zero credit risk. This is because the government generally fulfils its obligations. The same cannot be guaranteed in the case of corporate bonds.

a) Capital Protection

While no mutual fund offers 100% capital protection, gilt funds are one of the few that carry minimal risk. Investments are made in government-backed securities, and the chances of any significant capital loss are close to none.

b) Invest in Securities Not Available to Retail Investors

Most of the government securities are unavailable to retail investors. But, institutional investors like fund houses are allowed to subscribe to such securities. By investing in gilt funds, you get to invest in such government securities indirectly.

c) Reasonable Returns

As compared to many other investment options, gilt funds offer decent returns even if you are investing for short to medium term. Combined with the minimum risk, this is an excellent option for risk-averse investors.

Risks and Disadvantages of Investing in Gilt Funds

The biggest risk in gilt funds is that of the fluctuating interest rates. The returns can fall considerably if the RBI increases the repo rate. Apart from this, there is no significant risk of investing in gilt funds

Moreover, gilt funds are considered to be quite illiquid securities. This implies that if an investor wants to exit his position and liquidate his investments in case of an emergency, he won't be able to do so easily.

Balanced Funds

A balanced fund combines an equity stock component, a bond component and sometimes a money market component in a single portfolio. Generally, these hybrid funds stick to a relatively fixed mix of stocks and bonds that reflects either a moderate, or higher equity, component, or conservative, or higher fixed-income, component orientation

These funds invest in a mix of equities and debt, giving the investor the best of both worlds. Balanced funds gain from a healthy dose of equities but the debt portion fortifies them against any downturn.

Balanced funds are suitable for a medium-term horizon and are ideal for investors who are looking for a mixture of safety, income and modest capital appreciation. The amounts this type of mutual fund invests into each asset class usually must remain within a set minimum and maximum.

Features of balanced funds

1) Diversification

Balanced funds offer diversification within a single investment. This is because they invest in both stocks and bonds, spreading out risk across different asset classes.

2) Risk reduction

Balanced funds reduce investment risk by balancing exposure towards debt and equity.

3) Taxation benefits

Equity balanced funds generally have at least 65% of their corpus invested in stocks and qualify for the same tax treatment as equity funds.

4) Direct investments

Investors can purchase shares of balanced funds directly from the fund company or through a financial advisor.

5) Dynamic asset allocation funds

These funds invest in both debt and equity investment instruments and continually change their allocation as per the market conditions.

Monthly income Plan

Monthly Income Plans (MIPs) are hybrid funds; i.e. they invest in debt papers as well as equities. Investors who want a regular income stream invest in these schemes. The objective of these schemes is to provide regular income to the investor by paying dividends; however, there is no guarantee that these schemes will pay dividends every month. Investment in the debt portion provides for the monthly income whereas investment in the equities provides for the extra return 105 which is helpful in minimising the impact of inflation.

The following features and benefits of the best monthly income scheme make it a feasible investment option for risk-averse investors

a) *No limit:*

The scheme is flexible and does not come with any upper limit on its investment amount. It allows someone to invest in the scheme as per their capability and requirement.

b) *Open-ended option:*

Monthly Income Scheme is an open-ended scheme. Individuals do not have to pay any processing charges as an entry load for entering the said scheme. Additionally, it comes with an exit-load that is less than 1% of total sum of investment.

c) *Liquidity:*

An MIP scheme is more liquid when compared to most other schemes. As there is no lock-in period applicable on the investment, investors can choose to withdraw their funds to meet any unforeseen emergency.

d) *Better returns:*

Earnings generated through an MIP are better than that of traditional fixed deposits and Post Office Monthly Income Scheme.

e) *Guaranteed income:*

Investors are guaranteed to earn assured returns each month, despite the quantum of the sum varying depending on the financial market.

f) *Lower-risk:*

MIPs are associated with lower-risk components. It is because money is invested in low-risk securities like preferred shares, fixed-income instruments and dividend stocks.

g) *Professionally managed:*

MIP is managed by professional fund managers who are better equipped to understand the functioning of the investment market. They not just monitor schemes but also decide all the 'when, how, and how much' when it comes to switching funds to debts and equities.

Child benefit plan

These are debt oriented funds, with very little component invested into equities. The objective here is capital protection and steady appreciation as well. Parents can invest in these schemes with a 5 – 15 year horizon, so that they have adequate money when their children need it for meeting expenses related to higher education.

Liquid Mutual Funds

A Liquid Mutual Fund is a debt fund which invests in fixed-income instruments like commercial paper, government securities, treasury bills, etc. with a maturity of up to 91 days. The net asset value or NAV of a liquid fund is calculated for 365 days. Further, investors can get their withdrawals processed within 24 hours. These funds carry the lowest interest-rate risk in the debt funds category.

How do Liquid Mutual Funds work?

The core objective of a liquid fund is *providing capital protection and liquidity to the investors.* Therefore, the fund manager *selects high-quality debt securities and invests according to the scheme's mandate.*

Further, he ensures that the average maturity of the portfolio is not more than 91 days. Shorter maturity makes the fund less prone to change in interest rates.

By matching the maturity of individual securities with the maturity of the portfolio, the fund manager tries to deliver better returns. Liquid funds are known to offer better returns than a regular savings account.

Factors to consider before investing in Liquid Mutual Funds in India

Here are some important aspects that you must consider before investing in liquid funds in India:

a) *Risks*

Since the underlying assets of a liquid fund have a maturity of up to 91 days, they do not experience a lot of volatility. Hence, the NAV of the fund remains almost steady. This makes liquid funds low-risk investments.

However, it is important to note that if the credit rating of any underlying security drops, then the NAV can experience a drop too. Liquid funds are NOT risk-free.

b) _Returns_

A quick look at the performance of liquid funds will tell you that these funds offer around 7-9% returns on an average. Hence, they are better than the 4% returns earned on savings account deposits.

c) _Expense Ratio_

Like all other mutual fund schemes, liquid funds also charge an annual fee for offering fund management services. This is called expense ratio - a percentage of the total assets of the fund. Funds with a lower expense ratio are preferred by most debt investors as it helps in maximising their gains. Further, most fund managers of liquid funds invest and hold the security until maturity. Therefore, the fund does not incur expenses due to excessive buying and selling of securities keeping the expense ratio low.

d) _Investment Plan_

Liquid funds are used by many investors to create an emergency fund. They offer reasonable returns at lower risks and are as liquid as savings account deposits. These funds are designed for investors with a 3-month investment horizon. Hence, before investing in these funds, ensure that you create an investment plan accordingly.

Liquid mutual funds are schemes that make investments in debt and money market securities with maturity of up to 91 days only. In case of liquid mutual funds cut off time for receipt of funds is an important consideration.

As per SEBI guidelines the following cut-off timings shall be observed by a mutual fund in respect of purchase of units in liquid fund schemes and the following NAVs shall be applied for such purchase:

a) **where the application is received up to 2.00 p.m.** on a day and funds are available for utilisation before the cut-off time without availing any credit facility, whether, intra-day or otherwise – _the closing NAV of the day immediately preceding the day of receipt of application_

b) **where the application is received after 2.00 p.m.** on a day and funds are available for utilisation on the same day without availing any credit facility, whether, intra-day or otherwise – _the closing NAV of the day immediately preceding the next business day_

c) **Irrespective of the time of receipt of application,** where the funds are not available for utilisation before the cut-off time without availing any credit facility, whether intra-day or 106 otherwise – *the closing NAV of the day immediately preceding the day on which the funds are available for utilisation.*

Questions For Practice (MCQ)

1) _________________ are mutual fund units which investors buy/ sell from the stock exchange, as against a normal mutual fund unit

a) **ETF**

b) Equity shares

c) Preference shares

d) None of the above

2) ETFs have relatively _______ as compared to a mutual fund scheme.

a) **Less costly**

b) Costly

c) Cheaper

d) Same as mutual fund

3) The _______ provide two way quotes for the ETFs on the stock exchange

a) DP

b) **Authorised participant**

c) Custodian

d) Broker

4) An Exchange Traded Fund (ETF) is essentially a scheme where the investor has to buy/ sell units from the market through a ________

a) **Broker**

b) Sub-broker

c) Custodian

d) Depositary participant

5) While a typical Index fund would have expenses in the range of
________ of Net Assets

a) 1.75%

b) **1.5%**

c) 1.25%

d) 2.25%

6) RETIS __________ is bound to ensure compliance with applicable
laws and protect the rights of the unit holders.

a) **Trustee**

b) Custodian

c) Depositary

d) AMC

7) _______ gives equivalent number of units bundled together to
these authorised participants (AP)

a) **AMC**

b) Trustee

c) Sponsor

d) Custodian

8) The Gold which the AP deposits for buying the bundled ETF units
is known as __________

a) **Portfolio deposit**

b) Depositary

c) AMC

d) Sponser

9) An account is maintained for the purpose of depositing and
withdrawing of Gold , is known as ______________

a) **Allocated account**

b) Demat account

c) Portfolio account

d) Either a or b

10) A report is submitted by the___________, no later than the following business day, to the AMC.

a) **Custodian**

b) Depository

c) AMC

d) Board of directors

11) The money which the AP deposits for buying the bundled ETF units is known as ____________

a) Call money

b) **Cash components**

c) Application money

d) All of the above

12) Sovereign gold bonds issued by _________ on behalf of government of india

a) Reserve bank of india

b) SEBI

c) NSE

d) Department of Economic Affairs

13) The tenor of the Bond will be for a period of _________ with exit option from ______ to be exercised on the interest payment dates.

a) **8th year, 5th Year**

b) 5th year, 8th Year

c) 5th year, 7th Year

d) 8th year, 6th Year

14) The maximum amount subscribed by an entity will not be more than ________ per person

a) 500 grams

b) 1 kg

c) 2 kg

d) **4 kg**

15) Payment for the Bonds will be through cash payment upto a maximum of _________

a) 15000

b) **20000**

c) 25000

d) 30000

16) APs are like market makers and continuously offer _________

a) Buy price

b) Bid-ask spread

c) **Two way quote**

d) None of the above

17) The difference between two way quote is known as ______

a) Return

b) Profit

c) **Bid-ask spread**

d) All of the above

18) The difference between the returns given by Gold and those delivered by the scheme is known as _________

a) Profit

b) Loss

c) **Tracking error**

d) None of the above

19) _________risk can be reduced by adjusting the maturity of the debt fund portfolio

a) **Interest rate risk**

b) Credit risk

c) Fluctuation rate risk

d) Market risk

20) So, if the investor expects interest rates to rise, he would be better off giving _________

   a) **Short term loans**

   b) Long term loans

   c) Medium term loan

   d) All of the above

21) ____________ will be called as eight wonder of the world

   a) Simple interest

   b) Compound interest

   c) **Legal interset**

   d) Yearly interset

22) If an FMP is giving a relatively higher indicative yield, it may be investing in __________

   a) **Riskier security**

   b) Safest security

   c) Moderate risk security

   d) Moderate safe security

23) _________ is the return which investors can expect from the FMP.

   a) Simple interest

   b) Dividend

   c) **Indicative yield**

   d) Compound interset

24) indicative yields are _______

   a) Pre-tax

   b) Post-tax

   c) **Tax free**

   d) Investor have to bear tax after getting return

25) ____________ fund invest only in securities issued by the Government. This can be the Central Govt. or even State Govts.

a) FMP

b) Capital protection fund

c) Balanced fund

d) **Gilt fund**

26) Debt paper is having maturity of as low as _______

a) 3 months

b) One month

c) 1 year

d) Two months

27) In case of mutual fund , where the application is received up to 2.00 p.m. on a day and funds are available for utilisation before the cut-off time without availing any credit facility, whether, intra-day or otherwise the NAV will be taken as ______________

a) immediately preceding the next business day

b) **immediately preceding the day of receipt of application**

c) immediately preceding the day on which the funds are available for utilisation

d) None of the above

28) All money market and debt securities, including floating rate securities, with residual maturity of up to 60 days shall be valued at the ___________

a) Capitalisation method

b) Weighted average capital method

c) **Weighted average method**

d) Amortisation bases

29) ____________ will constantly change its portfolio.

a) Balanced fund

b) Mutual fund

c) Capital protection fund

d) **Liquid fund**

30) The stress test should be carried out internally at least _______

a) Every 6 months

b) **Every one month**

c) Every 3 month

d) Every year

31) The stress test should be reviewed by _______

a) Trustee

b) Sponser

c) Board of directors

d) **A and c**

32) The object of child protection fund is _________

a) To earn compound interest

b) Capital appreciation

c) Steady income

d) **Both b and c**

33) A Risk Free Benchmark Yield is built using the_________as the base

a) Central govt

b) Index

c) Market price

d) **Government securities**

34) Yield to Maturity (YTM), this is rate applied to the _________

a) Present value of cash flow

b) **Future value of cash flow**

c) To arrive at yearly interset

d) To arrive at bond pricing

35) _________ in liquid schemes happens more often due the short term nature of securities invested in.

a) Fixed interest rate

b) **Portfolio churning**

c) Fluctuation

d) Change in the portfolio deposit

36) _________ risk is also called risk of default

  a) **Credit risk**

  b) System risk

  c) Unsystematic risk

  d) None of the above

37) Globally there are ETF on _________

  a) Gold

  b) Silver

  c) Indices

  d) **All of the above**

38) Which of the standard characteristic the debt paper have

  a) Maturity

  b) Principal

  c) Interset

  d) **All of the above**

39) An interest rises, when NAV ____-

  a) **Fall**

  b) Rise

  c) Remain same

  d) Either fall or rise

Define the following

  1) ETF

  2) REITs

  3) Gold ETF

  4) Sovereign gold Bonds

  5) Fixed maturity plan

  6) Capital protection fund

  7) Gilt fund

  8) Balanced funds

  9) Monthly income plan

  10) Child benefits plan

  11) Liquid mutual funds

Short question

1) Explain any two types of ETF

2) Explain the salient features of ETF

3) Explain the features of Gold ETF

4) What are the advantages and disadvantages of Gold ETF

5) Explain the CRISIL and its types

6) Explain yield to maturity with example

7) Explain the advantages of fixed maturity plan

Short questions

a) Explain the working of Gold ETF

b) Who is the AP? What are the features of AP

c) Role of custodian in Gold-ETF

d) What is difference between coupon rate and yield to maturity

e) Explain the difference between interest rate risk and credit risk

f) What are the features of fixed maturity plan

g) How do liquid maturity Funds work?

h) Role of Custodian in Gold-ETF

Long questions

1) Being as an investor if you want to invest in any of the below funds, in which funds you will invest and why

    a) bond ETF

    b) Commodity ETF

    c) Equity fund

    d) Sectoral ETF

2) An investor invests in a number of investments and wants to earn the maximum return, according to you in which interest rate he will earn maximum interest compounding or simple interest and why? Explain with the help of an example?

3) What are the ways to reduce the interest rate risk and credit risk ?

Unit 5
Taxation and Regulations

Introduction

There was a major change in the taxation rules from 1 April 2023 onwards by Finance Act, 2023.

Before 1 April 2023, for the purpose of taxation, the Indian mutual fund universe is basically divided into fund categories- Equity Oriented Fund and Funds other than Equity Oriented Fund

1. Equity Oriented Fund- Schemes with at least 65% of the portfolio in Equity shares of domestic company listed on recognised stock exchange

2. Funds other than Equity Oriented Funds- Schemes with less than 65% exposure in Equity shares of domestic company listed on recognised stock exchange

Note – These categories are mentioned for understanding of taxation.

Let's take a detailed look at what is indexation in mutual funds, how it is calculated, changes to Long Term Capital Gains (LTCG) tax rules from 2023, and more-

How capital gain are taxed

Fund type	Short term capital gains	Long term capital gains
Equity type	15%+cess+surcharge	Up to Rs.one lakh tax exempt any gain above one lakh are taxed @10%+cess+surchage
Debt funds	Taxed at the investors income tax slab rate	20%+cess+surcharge

| Hybrid equity-oriented funds | 15%+cess+surcharge | Up to Rs.one lakh tax exempt any gain above one lakh are taxed @10%+cess+surchage |
| Hybrid debt oriented funds | Taxed at the investors income tax slab rate | 20%+cess+surcharge |

➡️ *Indexation Definition*

Indexation refers to modifying a price, or any other value in accordance with changes in another price or a composite indicator of prices.

Indexation is used to make adjustments in the purchase price of an investment to reflect the effect of inflation on it.

With the help of indexation, you can index (adjust or inflate) the cost of the acquisition of an asset over a period of time to bring it to the current prices after considering the impact of inflation. Indexation is done using a Price Index and this price index is adjusted for indexation. It is adjusted for indexation at the time of buying and selling an asset.

What is Indexation in Mutual Funds?

Redemption or sale of Investments in mutual funds create capital gains. Capital gains can be either long-term or short-term depending upon the holding period. The taxation component depends upon the type of mutual fund. and date of purchase.

On investments before 1 April 2023, Indexation benefit was applicable for capital gains generated in mutual funds other than Equity oriented Funds .

When it comes to taxation of Funds other than Equity oriented Funds before 1 April 2023, you generate STCG (Short-Term Capital Gains) if the holding period is less than 36 months. If the investment is held for 36 months or more, you generate LTCG (Long-Term Capital Gains).

STCG from such Funds is added to the investor's taxable income and is taxed as per their tax slab.

On the other hand, LTCG is taxed at 20% but used to come with indexation tax benefits. With indexation, the cost of acquiring or purchasing units of the debt scheme used to be adjusted for inflation to reduce the tax liability.

Before we get started lets understand....

Income tax slab rates for FY 2023-24/ AY 2024-25			
Old Regime			
Slabs	Individuals (Age < 60 years)	Resident Senior Citizens ($\geq$60 but <80 years)	Resident Super Senior Citizens (80 years and above)
Up to Rs 2,50,000	Nil	Nil	Nil
Rs 2,50,001 to Rs 3,00,000	5%	Nil	Nil
Rs 3,00,001 to Rs 5,00,000	5%	5%	Nil
Rs 5,00,001 to Rs 10,00,000	20%	20%	20%
Above Rs 10,00,000	30%	30%	30%
New Regime			
Slabs	Income Tax Rates		
Up to Rs 3,00,000	Nil		
Rs 3,00,001 to Rs 6,00,000	5% (Tax rebate u/s 87A)		
Rs 6,00,001 to Rs 900,000	10% (Tax rebate u/s 87A up to Rs 7 lakh)		
Rs 9,00,001 to Rs 12,00,000	15%		
Rs 12,00,001 to Rs 1500,000	20%		
Above Rs 15,00,000	30%		

a) If you sell an asset such as bonds, shares, mutual fund units, property etc; you must pay tax on the profit earned from it.

b) This profit is called Capital Gains.

c) The tax paid on this capital gains is called Capital Gains Tax.

d) If you sell the asset after 36 months from the date of purchase (12 months for Equity Shares and Equity Mutual Funds), it is called Long Term Capital Gains.

Income Tax laws have a provision of reducing the effective tax burden on long term capital gains that you earn.

- This provision allows you to _increase the purchase price of the asset_ that you have sold.

- This _reduces the profit gap between purchase price and sale price_ which in turn reduces the net tax payable as the "tax" is a function of the profit gap.

- The idea behind this provision is inflation, _it reduces asset value over a period of time._

- This benefit provided by Income Tax laws is called 'Indexation'

- Under Indexation, you are allowed by law _to inflate the purchase price of your asset by a government notified inflation factor._

- This factor is _called the 'Cost Inflation Index,_ from which the word 'Indexation' has been derived.

This inflation index is used to _artificially inflate the purchase price of your asset price so that it reflects its true value in the year of taxation._

Cost of Inflation Index for FY 2023-24 AY 2024-25 for Capital Gain with base year 2001-02

(www.basunivesh.com)

Financial Year (FY)	Assessment Year (AY)	Cost of Inflation Index (CII)
2001-02	2002-03	100
2002-03	2003-04	105
2003-04	2004-05	109
2004-05	2005-06	113
2005-06	2006-07	117
2006-07	2007-08	122
2007-08	2008-09	129
2008-09	2009-10	137
2009-10	2010-11	148
2010-11	2011-12	167
2011-12	2012-13	184
2012-13	2013-14	200
2013-14	2014-15	220
2014-15	2015-16	240
2015-16	2016-17	254
2016-17	2017-18	264
2017-18	2018-19	272
2018-19	2019-20	280
2019-20	2020-21	289
2020-21	2021-22	301
2021-22	2022-23	317
2022-23	2023-24	331
2023-24	2024-25	348

For Example

- An asset was purchased in FY 2001-02 for Rs. 2.50 lacs
- This asset was sold in FY 2004-05 for Rs. 4.50 lacs
- Cost Inflation Index in 2001-02 was 100
- Cost Inflation Index in 2004-05 was 113

So, indexed cost of acquisition would be:

Rs. 2.50,000 X113/100

= Rs.282500

Selling Price of an asset — Indexed Cost = Capital Gains

i.e. 4,50,000 - Rs. 282500 = Rs. 167500

Therefore tax payable will be 20% of Rs. 167500 which comes to Rs. 33500

Rahul purchased a flat in FY 2001-02 for Rs. 10,00,000. He sells the flat in FY 2017-18 at 30,00,000 What will be the indexed cost of acquisition?

In this case, CII for the year 2001-02 and 2017-18 is 100 and 272 respectively.

Hence, the indexed cost of acquisition = 10,00,000 x 272/100 = Rs. 27,20,000

FII:- Not availing indexation benefit then tax will be 10%(30,00,000-10,00,000)=2,00,000

Resident= availing the indexation benefit=(30,00,000-27,20,000)=280000

20% on 2,80,000=560000

Case 2:

Shivani purchased a capital asset in FY 1995-1996 for Rs. 2,00,000. FMV of the capital asset on 1st April 2001 was Rs. 3,20,000. She sells the asset in FY 2016-17 for Rs.8,00,000

What is the indexed cost of acquisition?

Here, the asset is purchased before the base year.

Hence the cost of acquisition = Higher of the actual cost or FMV on 1st April 2001. i.e. cost of acquisition = Rs. 3,20,000.

CII for the year 2001-02 and 2016-17 is 100 and 264 respectively.

Indexed cost of acquisition = 3,20,000 x 264/100 = Rs. 8,44,800

Calculation of tax 20% on (Rs. 8,44,800 – Rs.8,00,000) =8960

Case 3:

Gita has purchased equity shares of Rs.1,00,000 on 1st March 2015 and sells the shares at Rs.1,20,000 on 1st April 2020. What will be the indexed cost of acquisition?

CII for the year of purchase FY 2014-15 is 240 and

for the year of sale 2020-21 is 301

Hence, indexed cost of acquisition = Rs.1,00,000 x 301/240 = Rs.1,25,416

Calculation of tax 20% on (1,25.416 - Rs.1,20,000 =5416) =1084

(Assume that investor fall in the last category of tax slab)

The CII (Cost of Inflation Index) was used for adjusting the purchase price in the case of LTCG from funds other than Equity oriented Funds. The Finance Ministry releases CII figures for every financial year. Here are the steps to calculate adjusted LTCG

1. The CII of the year when the units were sold was divided by the CII of the year when they were purchased and multiplied by the initial purchase cost..

2. The adjusted cost was deducted from the selling price and multiplied by the total number of units to calculate the LTCG.

Equity schemes

a) As per SEBI Regulations, any scheme which has minimum 65% of its average weekly net assets invested in Indian equities, is an equity scheme.

b) If the mutual fund units of an equity scheme are sold / redeemed / repurchased after 12 months, the profit is exempt.

c) However if units are sold before 12 months it results in short term capital gain. The investor has to pay 15% as short term capital gains tax. While exiting the scheme, the investor will have to bear a Securities Transaction Tax (STT) @ 0.001% of the value of selling price.

DIVIDEND DISTRIBUTION TAX

The dividend declared by mutual funds *in respect of the various schemes is exempt from tax in the hands of investors.*

a) In case of debt mutual funds, **the AMCs are required to pay Dividend Distribution Tax** (DDT) from the distributable income.

This ensures ease in tax collection. However, in case of equity funds no DDT is payable. The rates for DDT are as follows:

b) For Individuals and HUF – 25% (plus surcharge and other cess as applicable)

For others – 30% (plus surcharge and other cess as applicable)

c) On dividend distributed to a non-resident or to a foreign company by an Infrastructure Debt Fund – 5% (plus surcharge and other cess as applicable)

FIXED MATURITY PLAN

A Fixed Maturity Plan (FMP) is a type of closed-ended mutual fund that invests in debt instruments. FMPs have fixed tenures, and automatically redeem investments on a specific date.

Here are some features of FMPs:

a) Lock-in period

FMPs have a lock-in period that prevents funds from being withdrawn during the tenure. This is to ensure that the deposit remains locked-in for the given tenure to generate maximum returns from the underlying securities.

b) Tax implications

Returns from FMPs are subject to tax. If investors choose the "dividend" option, they are subject to a 12.5% dividend distribution tax (DDT) plus applicable surcharge and cess. However, for 3 year FMPs, there is only capital gains where you pay tax at 20% after indexation.

c) Interest rate

Because the rate of returns associated with FMPs are fixed, they are hardly exposed to interest rate-related risks.

Particulars	With Indexation	Without Indexation
Amount Invested (Rs)	100000	100000
Tenor (in days)	372	372
Indicative Yield	7%	7%
Total Amount + Interest (Rs)	107138.93	107138.93
Interest/Gain (Rs)	7138.93	7138.93
Indexed Cost (Rs)	106000	-
Indexed Gain (Rs)	1138.93	-
Tax Rates	22.66%	11.33%
Tax Amount (Rs)	258.08	808.84
Post Tax Gain (Rs)	6880.85	6330.09
Post Tax Yield (Rs)	6.75	6.21

(For a one-year FMP, the tax works out to 10% without indexation and 20% with indexation. Indexation benefit for FMPs are high, since the inflation rate is high, as a result, you may have to pay less tax for an FMP)

Other features of FMPs include:

- **Fixed tenure**
- **Investment strategy**
- **Sensitivity to interest rates**

- **Credit risk**

- **Balancing of portfolio**

What are the benefits of FMP

a) *Minimal Risk:* Debt funds, are exposed to three kinds of risks viz. interest rate risk, credit risk and liquidity risk. FMPs are designed to effectively minimise and in some case eliminate these risks.

b) *Interest Rate Risk:* FMPs are least exposed to interest rate risk as the fund manager holds the instruments till maturity getting a fixed rate of return like a normal FD.

c) *Credit Risk:* FMPs primarily invest in AAA or P1+ rated instruments with a short-term maturity profile from 3 months to 36 months and thus there are very low/ no credit risks.

d) *Liquidity Risk:* High credit quality automatically ensures high liquidity too.This effectively means that investors can protect themselves from any capital loss on maturity.

e) *Low Expenses:* FMPs because of their very nature of holding the instrument till maturity, FMPs minimises expenses. Unlike a bond fund, there is no redemption pressure and as there is also no regular churning of the portfolio, this reduces costs incurred in buying these instruments and the fund managers cost of reviewing the portfolio on a regular basis.

f) *Liquidity:* Although FMP is best if held till maturity, but investors have an option to exit at any point as all FMPs are traded.

Differences between FMPs and FDs

The differences between the FMPs and FDs are mentioned in the below table:

Parameter	FMP	FD (Fixed deposit)
1) Return	Indicative, not assured	Guaranteed, fixed
2) Tax	Dividend option: DDT tax Growth option: Capital gains tax with indexation benefit	Interest income is taxed as per the slab rate

3) Liquidity	Restricted, close-ended	High, premature withdrawal is possible
4) Risk	Moderate, subject to market fluctuations	Low, backed by deposit insurance
5) Expense Ratio	Low, buy and hold strategy	Nil

WHAT ARE THE GUIDELINES FOR INVESTMENT IN SCHEMES

1. No scheme can invest _more than 10% of its NAV in rated debt instruments of a single issuer wherein the limit is reduced to 10% of NAV_ which may be extended to 12% of NAV with the prior approval of the Board of Trustees and the Board of Asset Management Company.

2. No scheme _can invest more than 10% of its NAV in unrated paper of a single issuer_ and total investment by any scheme in unrated papers cannot exceed 25% of the NAV.

3. No mutual fund _scheme shall invest more than 30% in money market instruments_ of an issuer: Provided that such limit shall not be applicable for investments in Government securities, treasury bills and collateralized borrowing and lending obligations.

4. No fund, under _all its schemes can hold more than 10% of company's paid up capital carrying voting rights._

5. No scheme can invest _more than 10% of its NAV in equity shares_ or equity related instruments of **any company of a single company.** Provided that, the limit of 10% shall not be applicable for investments in case of index fund or sector or industry specific scheme.

6. If a scheme invests _in another scheme of the same or different AMC, no fees will be charged._ Aggregate inter scheme investment cannot exceed 5% of net asset value of the mutual fund.

7. _No scheme can invest in unlisted securities_ of its sponsor or its group entities.

8. Schemes can _invest in unlisted securities issued by entities other than the sponsor or sponsor's group._ Open ended schemes can invest maximum of 5% of net assets in such securities whereas close ended schemes can invest up-to 10% of net assets in such securities.

9. Schemes _cannot invest in listed entities belonging to the sponsor group beyond 25%_ of its net assets.

10. _**Total exposure of debt schemes of mutual funds**_ in a particular sector (excluding investments in Bank CDs, CBLO, G-Secs, T Bills, short term deposits of scheduled commercial banks and AAA rated securities issued by Public Financial Institutions and Public Sector Banks) _**shall not exceed 25% of the net assets**_ of the scheme. An _**additional exposure to financial services sector not exceeding 5%**_ of the net assets of the scheme shall be allowed only by way of increase in exposure to Housing Finance Companies (HFCs) for HFCs rated AA and above and registered with National Housing Bank (NHB).

11. _**Total exposure of debt schemes of mutual funds in a group**_ (excluding investments in securities issued by Public Sector) _**shall not exceed 20% of the net assets**_ of the scheme. Such investment limit _**may be extended to 25% of the net assets of the scheme with the prior approval of the Board of Trustees**_

➡ _**What is the name of Industry Association for the Mutual Fund Industry?**_

AMFI (Association of Mutual Funds in India) is the industry association for the mutual fund industry in India which was incorporated in the year 1995.

What are the Objectives of AMFI?

a) _Regulate the mutual fund industry_

AMFI's role is to regulate the mutual fund industry, including the conduct of distributors. AMFI also issues ARN (All India Registry Number) to eligible participants after certification.

b) _Promote investor education_

AMFI's role is to promote investor education and ensure the smooth functioning of the market.

c) _Set ethical standards_

AMFI's role is to promote the investors' interest by defining and maintaining high ethical and professional standards in the mutual fund industry.

d) _Protect investor interests_

AMFI's role is to protect the interests of investors and unit holders. Investors can issue complaints to AMFI regarding misuse of money or lack of transparency from Asset Management Companies (AMCs).

e) *Recommend business practices*

AMFI's role is to recommend and promote best business practices and code of conduct to be followed by members and others engaged in mutual fund and asset management activities.

In March 2013, SEBI introduced the concept of 'product labelling' for the MF industry.

The move was aimed at helping investors interpret the inherent risk associated with a scheme through easy-to-understand colour code boxes.

In the initial phase, the product labelling system used three colours — blue - to denote low-risk, yellow – to represent medium risk and brown – to denote high risk.

Accordingly, all fund houses shall display the product label including colour code boxes depicting the levels of risk, in all scheme related documents and advertisements.

Effective January 01, 2021, level of risk depicted by a pictorial meter (known as a riskometer) as under:

- Low - Principal at low risk

- Low to Moderate - Principal at moderately low risk

- Moderate - Principal at moderate risk

- Moderately High - Principal at moderately high risk

- High - Principal at high risk

- Very High – Principle at a very high risk

How are the risks categorised?

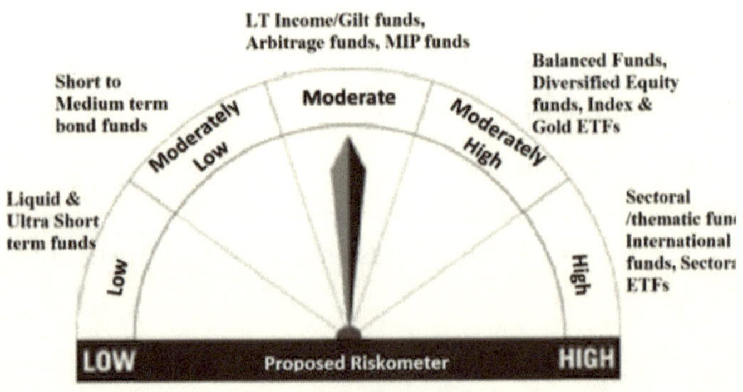

Previously, the riskometer had five levels of risk – Low, Moderately Low, Moderate, Moderately High and High.

RISKOMETER

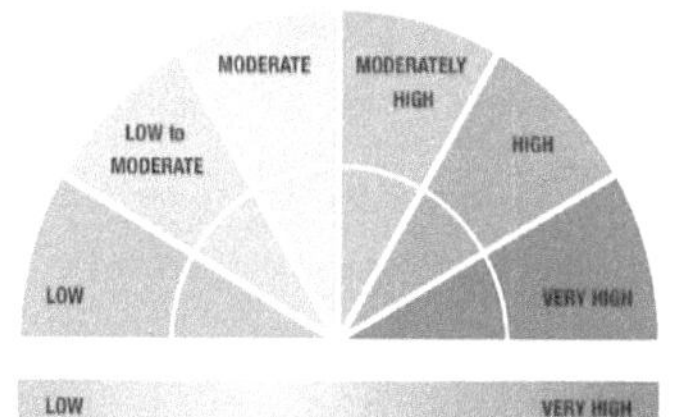

Risk Level Suitable For Investor Profile

- A Low Conservative Investor is _willing to accept minimal risks_ and hence, might receive _minimum or no returns_.

- Low to Moderate Moderately Conservative Investor is willing to accept a small level of risk in exchange for some potential _returns over the medium to long term._

- Moderate investors can tolerate moderate levels of risk in exchange for relatively higher potential returns over the _medium to long term._

- Moderately High Moderately Aggressive Investor is keen to accept higher level of risk in order to _maximise potential returns over the medium to long termination_

- A High Aggressive Investor is willing to accept significant risks to maximise potential returns over the long term and _is aware that he/ she may lose all or significant part of capital._

- Very High Very Aggressive Investor is willing to accept very high risks to maximise potential returns over the long term and is aware that he/she may lose all/ significant part of capital.

ADVANTAGES OF MUTUAL FUND

1. _Professional Management —_

Investors may not have the time or the required knowledge and resources to conduct their research and purchase individual stocks or bonds.

A mutual fund is managed by full-time, professional money managers who have the expertise, experience and resources to actively buy, sell, and monitor investments. A fund manager continuously monitors investments and rebalances the portfolio accordingly to meet the scheme's objectives. Portfolio management by professional fund managers is one of the most important advantages of a mutual fund.

2. _Risk Diversification —_

Buying shares in a mutual fund is an easy way to diversify your investments across many securities and asset categories such as equity, debt and gold, which helps in spreading the risk - so you won't have all your eggs in one basket. This proves to be beneficial when an underlying security of a given mutual fund scheme experiences market headwinds. With diversification, the risk associated with one asset class is countered by the others.

Even if one investment in the portfolio decreases in value, other investments may not be impacted and may even increase in value. In other words, you don't lose out on the entire value of your investment if a particular component of your portfolio goes through a turbulent period. Thus, risk diversification is one of the most prominent advantages of investing in mutual funds.

3. *Affordability & Convenience (Invest Small Amounts)* —

For many investors, it could be more costly to directly purchase all of the individual securities held by a single mutual fund. By contrast, the minimum initial investments for most mutual funds are more affordable.

4. *Liquidity* —

You can easily redeem (liquidate) units of open ended mutual fund schemes to meet your financial needs on any business day (when the stock markets and/or banks are open), so you have easy access to your money. Upon redemption, the redemption amount is credited in your bank account within one day to 3-4 days, depending upon the type of scheme e.g., in respect of Liquid Funds and Overnight Funds, the redemption amount is paid out the next business day.

However, please note that units of close-ended mutual fund schemes can be redeemed only on maturity. Likewise, units of ELSS have a 3-year lock-in period and can be liquidated only thereafter.

5. *Low Cost* —

An important advantage of mutual funds is their low cost. Due to huge economies of scale, mutual funds schemes have a low expense ratio. Expense ratio represents the annual fund operating expenses of a scheme, expressed as a percentage of the fund's daily net assets. Operating expenses of a scheme are administration, management, advertising related expenses, etc. The limits of expense ratio for various types of schemes has been specified under Regulation 52 of SEBI Mutual Fund Regulations, 1996.

6. *Well-Regulated*

Mutual Funds are regulated by the capital markets regulator, Securities and Exchange Board of India (SEBI) under SEBI (Mutual Funds) Regulations,

1996. SEBI has laid down stringent rules and regulations keeping investor protection, transparency with appropriate risk mitigation framework and fair valuation principles.

7. *Tax Benefits*

Investment in ELSS up to ₹1,50,000 qualifies for tax benefit under section 80C of the Income Tax Act, 1961. Mutual Fund investments when held for a longer term are tax efficient.

Systematic Investment plan

A Systematic Investment Plan, commonly known as SIP is where regular fixed amounts are invested in your preferred Mutual Fund scheme. A Fixed amount is deducted each month from your savings account which is invested in the Mutual Fund of your choice.

Advantages of investing in SIP:

Here is a look at the advantages of investing in SIP:

a) *Simplicity of choice*

With SIP, you can start investing small amounts as small as Rs 500 each month and watch it grow. A SIP is not only simple and convenient to track, but also makes you save more.

b) *Rupee Cost Averaging:*

The unique feature of SIP is the Rupee Cost Averaging, where you buy more units when the market is low and buy less when the market is high. This is because of the inherent feature of SIP, where at every market correction, you will buy more, reducing your cost of investment and higher gains.

c) *Flexibility:-*

SIP provides you with tremendous flexibility. Long-term commitments like investing in instruments like Public Provident Fund or Unit Linked Insurance Plans can be avoided with SIP. These are open ended funds to be withdrawn as per your choice, meaning they do not have a fixed tenor. You can either withdraw the full or a partial amount from your investment, without incurring any losses. The amount of investment is also flexible: it can be increased or decreased. Just remember to have a long investment horizon for wealth creation.

d) *Higher returns:*

As compared to traditional fixed deposits or recurring deposits, SIP provides double the returns. This can help you beat the inflated costs.

e) _Power of compounding:_

SIP operates on the principle of receiving compound interest on your investments. In other words, a small amount invested for a long time fetches better returns than a one-time investment.

f) _Acts as an emergency fund:_

Being an open-ended fund without any tenor, you can withdraw your SIP Investment as a contingent fund.

➡ One-time investment vs SIP: Which is better?

If you are confused between one-time investment or SIP, refer to the comparison chart below:

	SIP investment	**One-time investment**
Tenor	Can be withdrawn anytime without any monetary loss.	Sudden withdrawal might attract charges, penalties, or might just not be allowed.
Earnings	Earns better during market lows. Investment yields higher returns because of the power of compounding.	Earns better during market highs. The investment yields fixed income, which is lower than SIP.
Protection from market volatility	SIP can protect your investment from any potential market crash.	One-time investment is not cushioned against market volatility. As such, this investment could be a major loss, if the market crashes.
Knowledge of market	This is a simple plan, and you do not require to have a thorough knowledge of the market.	In many cases, one-time investments may either require expert counsel, or a thorough knowledge of the market.

How to invest in SIP?

a) Identify your financial and investment goal:

First of all, you should identify your investment goal--whether it is wealth creation for short-term, medium-term or long-term. Start investing in SIP as per your goal. Remember that longer duration SIP yields higher returns.

b) <u>Select the right Mutual Fund:</u>

You must shortlist the right SIP mutual fund which is in the loop with your financial goals. You can compare different SIPs, and select the best.

c) <u>Contact the financial institution:</u>

Inform the financial company about your decision to invest in the specific SIP and fill the requisite form to complete <u>KYC documentation.</u>

d) <u>Invest:</u>

When your research is complete and you're ready to make an informed decision,Invest in your preferred SIP. You can do so with the help of an online demat account, to help simplify the process.

Thus, SIP stands for minimum investments and maximum returns. Invest in an SIP now and reap the returns later!

A Systematic Transfer Plan

A Systematic Transfer Plan enables investors to provide consent to a mutual fund to systematically transfer a certain amount or redeem certain units from one scheme and invest in an alternative scheme of the same mutual fund house.

Thus, at regular intervals an amount or number of units chosen by an individual investor is transferred from one mutual fund scheme to another of his or her choice. This facility thereby assists in deploying funds at regular intervals. In other words, it can be said that this is an automated way of moving money from one mutual fund to another. This plan is preferred when an individual is interested in investing a lump sum amount but wants to avoid the market timing risk. The most intelligent way of doing Systematic Transfer Plan is by transferring money from a debt fund to an equity fund.

What are some of the features of Systematic Transfer Plan?

Some of the features are as follows:

1. No standard minimum investment amount is required.

2. Systematic Transfer Plan enables a disciplined and lucrative transfer of funds.

3. Returns in Systematic Transfer Plan is higher as compared to that in bank savings account.

What are some of the benefits of Systematic Transfer Plan?

Some of the benefits of Systematic Transfer Plan include Rupee Cost Averaging, scope for higher return, earning steady returns, risk management and portfolio rebalancing.

Example Let's say an investor has decided to invest Rs 5,000 every month, such that Rs. 1,000 gets invested on the 5th, 10th, 15th, 20th and 25th of the month. This means that the Rs.5000, which will get invested in stages till 25th will remain in the savings account of the investor for 25 days and earn interest @ 4-6%, depending on the bank. If the investor moves this amount of Rs.5000 at the beginning of the month to a Liquid Fund and transfers Rs.1000 on the given dates to the scheme of his choice, then not only will he get the 117 benefit of SIP, but he will earn slightly higher interest as well in the Liquid Funds as compared to a bank FD. As the money is being invested in a Liquid Fund, the risk level associated is also minimal. Add to this the fact that liquid funds do not have any e xit loads. This is known as STP.

Systematic withdrawal plan

SWP stands for Systematic Withdrawal Plan. Here the investor invests a lump sum amount and withdraws some money regularly over a period of time.

This results in a steady income for the investor while at the same time his principal also gets drawn down gradually.

Say for example:-

An investor aged 60 years receives Rs.20 lakh at retirement. If he wants to use this money over a 20 year period, he can withdraw Rs. 20,00,000/20 = Rs.1,00,000 per annum. This translates into Rs.8,333 per month. (The investor will also get return on his investment of Rs.20 lakh, depending on where the money has been invested by the mutual fund).

In this example we have not considered the effect of compounding. If that is considered, then he will be able to either draw some more money every month, or he can get the same amount of Rs.8,333 per month for a longer period of time.

Note:-The conceptual difference between SWP and MIP is that SWP is an investment style whereas MIP is a type of scheme. In SWP the investor's capital goes down whereas in MIP, the capital is not touched and only the interest is paid to the investor as dividend.

Growth Option

Growth option is for those investors who are looking for capital appreciation. Say an investor aged 25 invests Rs.1 lakh in an equity scheme. He would not be requiring a regular income from his investment as his salary can be used for meeting his monthly expenses. He would instead want his money to grow and this can happen only if he remains invested for a long period of time. Such an investor should go for Growth option.

The NAV will fluctuate as the market moves. So if the scheme delivers a return of 12% after 1 year, his money would have grown by Rs.12,000. Assuming that he had invested at a NAV of Rs.100, then after 1 year the NAV would have grown to Rs.112.

Notice here that neither is any money coming out of the scheme, nor is the investor getting more units. His units will remain at 1,000 (1,00,000/ 100) which he bought when he invested Rs.1 lakh @ Rs. 100/ unit.

Dividend Payout Option

In case an investor chooses a Dividend Payout option, then after 1 year he would Receive Rs. 12 as dividend. This results in a cash outflow from the scheme. The impact of this would be that the NAV would fall by Rs.12 (to Rs. 100 after a year. In the growth option the NAV became Rs. 112) . Here he will not get any more number of units (they remain at 1,000), but will receive Rs.12,000 118 as dividend (Rs.12 per unit * 1,000 units). Dividend Payout will not give him the benefit of compounding as Rs.12,000 would be taken out of the scheme and will not continue to grow like money which is still invested in the scheme.

Dividend Reinvestment Option

In case of the Dividend Reinvestment option, the investor chooses to reinvest the dividend in the scheme.

So the Rs.12, which he receives as dividend gets invested into the scheme again @ Rs.100. This is because after payment of dividend, the NAV would fall to Rs.100. Thus the investor gets Rs.12,000/ Rs. 100 = 120 additional units.

> Mutual fund investors who don't want to take their dividend payouts can choose from either a growth option or a dividend reinvestment option.
>
> With a growth option, the investor lets the fund company invest the dividend payments in more securities and ultimately grow their money.
>
> With dividend reinvestments, fund managers are allowed to use dividend payments to buy more shares in the fund on behalf of the investor.
>
> Individual retirement account (IRA)

Notice here that although the investor has got 120 units more, the NAV has come down to Rs.100. Hence the return in case of all the three options would be the same. For Growth Option, the investor will have 100 units @ 112, which equals to Rs.1,12,000 while for Dividend Reinvested Option the investor will have 1120 units @ Rs. 100 which again amounts to Rs. 1,12,000.

Thus it can be seen that _there is no difference in either Growth or Dividend Reinvestment Plan._ It must be noted that for equity schemes there is no Dividend Distribution Tax, however for debt schemes, investor will not get Rs.12 as dividend, but less due to Dividend Distribution Tax.

In case of Dividend Reinvestment Option, he will get a slightly lesser number of units and not exactly 120 to the extent of Dividend Distribution Tax. In the case of Dividend Payout option the investor will lose out on the power of compounding from the second year onwards.

Question For Practice (MCQ)

1) There was a major change in taxation rule from ____________

   a) **1 April 2023**

   b) 30th April 2023

   c) 31st march 2023

   d) 1st january 2023

2) The equity type short term capital gains are taxed as________

   a) **15%+cess & surcharge**

   b) 5%+cess & surcharge

   c) 20%%+cess & surcharge

   d) Up to Rs.one lakh tax exempt any gain above one lakh are taxed @10%+cess+surchage

3) The debt funds are taxed as per ______

   a) 15%+cess+surcharge

   b) Taxed at the investor slab rate

   c) 20% +cess + surchage

   d) **Non- taxable**

4) Redemption or sale of investment in mutual fund creates ________

   a) Short term capital gain

   b) Long term capital gain

   c) **Either a or b**

   d) None of the above

5) If the investment other than equity held for _________ will be considered short term capital gain

a) Less than 12 months

b) **Less than 36 months**

c) More than 12 months

d) More than 36 months

6) ___________was used for adjusting the purchase price in case of LTCG from the funds other than Equity oriented funds

a) **CII**

b) Tax slab rate

c) Simple interest rate

d) Compound interest rate

7) The dividend declared by mutual fund is ______

a) Taxable as per tax slab

b) Taxable as per indexation

c) Taxable as per scheme

d) **Exempt from tax**

8) Debt funds are exposed to three kinds of risks viz. interest rate risk, credit risk and ___________

a) Market risk

b) Price risk

c) **Liquidity risk**

d) Systematic risk

9) FMPs primarily invest in AAA or P1+ rated instruments with a short-term maturity profile from 3 months to 36 months and thus there are __________

a) Very high risk

b) Moderate risk

c) **Very low/ no credit risks.**

d) No risk

10) High credit quality automatically ensures _________.This effectively means that investors can protect themselves from any capital loss on maturity.

a) Low liquidity

b) **High liquidity**

c) No liquidity

d) Either a or b

11) The dividend distribution tax is _____________ for individuals and HUF

a) **25% (plus surcharge and other cess as applicable)**

b) 5% (plus surcharge and other cess as applicable)

c) 15% (plus surcharge and other cess as applicable)

d) As per tax slab rate

12) No mutual fund scheme shall invest ____________ instruments of an issuer

a) **More than 30% in money market**

b) More than 10% of its NAV in equity shares

c) 5% of net asset value of the mutual fund.

d) None of the above

13) Schemes cannot invest in listed entities belonging to the _________ group beyond 25% of its net assets.

a) Trustee

b) **Sponser**

c) Board of directors

d) Amc

14) AMFI is incorporated in the year _______

a) **1995**

b) 1996

c) 1998

d) 2000

15) ________ has a role to regulate the mutual fund industry, including the conduct of distributors.

a) AMC

b) **AMFI**

c) TRUSTEE

d) SEBI

16) ___________ product labelling will show low risk

a) Brown

b) **Blue**

c) Yellow

d) Orange

17) An important advantage of mutual fund is ________

a) Well regulated

b) Tax benefits

c) **Low price risk**

d) Professionally managed

18) The unique feature of SIP is the ___________ where you buy more units when the market is low and buy less when the market is high.

a) Flexibility

b) Higher returns

c) **Rupee Cost Averaging,**

d) Power of compounding

19) ___________ investment plan will help investor to transfer certain amount or redeem certain amount from one scheme and invest in alternative scheme

a) SIP

b) **STP**

c) SWP

d) Child benefit plan

20) ___________is for those investor who are looking for capital appreciation

a) Dividend payout option

b) Dividend reinvestment option

c) **Growth option**

d) All of the above

21) Product labelling concept was issued in the year ______

a) March 2014

b) **March 2013**

c) March 2012

d) March 2010

22) Under Equity Mutual Fund, the holding period of long term capital gain is ______

a) Less than 12 months

b) **More than 12 months**

c) More than 36 months

d) Less than 36 months

23) __________ is a procedure by which the investor can get benefit from the fact that inflation has eroded his return

a) Dividend distribution tax

b) Both a or b

c) **Indexation**

d) None of the above

Define the following

1) *Indexation benefit*

2) *Short term capital gain*

3) *Long term capital gain*

4) *Fixed maturity plan*

5) *Systematic investment plan*

6) *Systematic transfer plan*

7) *Growth option*

Short questions

1) *Explain the features of fixed maturity plan*

2) *What are the benefits of fixed maturity plan*

3) *Explain the equity scheme along with the tax rate as long term and short term capital gain*

4) *What are the advantages of Systematic investment plan*

Short question

1) *How to invest in SIP?*

2) *What is the difference between the SIP and SWP*

3) *What are the features of SWP?*

4) *Explain the tax implication of equity scheme*

Long questions

1) *What are the guidelines for the investment in schemes*

2) *Which investment plan is better for investors from the following and why?*

   a) *One time investment plan*

   b) *SIP*

3) *If I need to invest for capital appreciation in which investment will I invest and why ?*

Unit 6
Quantitative Evaluation of Mutual Fund

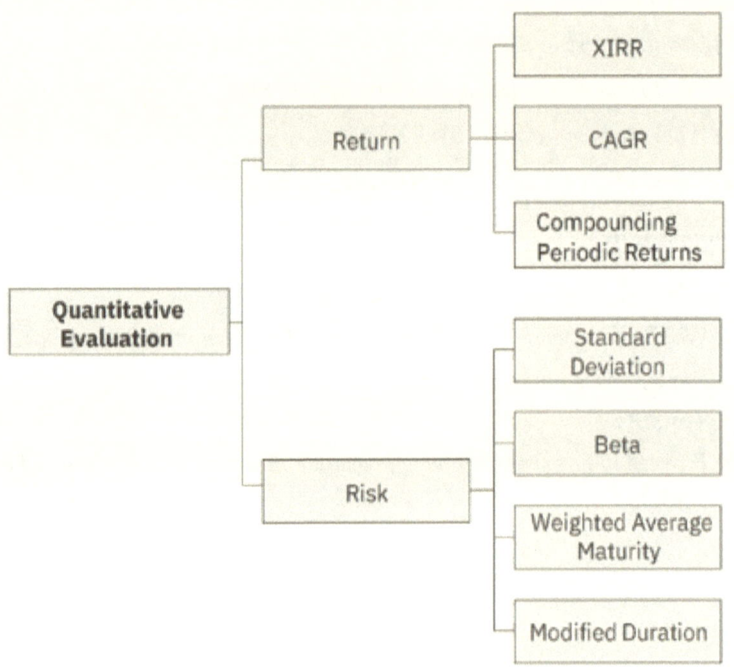

✗ *XIRR*

XIRR stands for ***Extended Internal Rate of Return.*** It's a financial metric that calculates the rate of return on investments based on their cash flows.

XIRR is a mathematical formula that measures the annualised return on investments that involve investments made and returns received at multiple time intervals.

What is XIRR in Mutual Funds: Meaning & How to Calculate

XIRR, also known as the ***Extended Internal Rate of Return,*** is a metric used to calculate the return on investment for mutual fund investments.

It is a mathematical formula used to measure the annualised return on investments that involve investments made and returns received at multiple time intervals.

The XIRR meaning is the returns earned by you over a period of time, and amount of all cash inflows/outflows, including dividends, capital gains, etc.

XIRR is the single rate of return that, when applied to every instalment, would give the current value of the total investment. It can be used for multiple cash flows, such as SIP, SWP, additional purchases, dividends, and partial redemptions.

XIRR is suitable for evaluating the performance of investments like SIPs, where contributions may not be consistent. It provides a more accurate measure of the annualised return, accounting for the timing and amount of each cash flow.

To calculate XIRR in Excel, you can:

- **Enter all your transactions in one column.**

- **Mark all outflows like investments and purchases as negative.**

- **Mark all inflows like redemptions as positive.**

- **In the last row, enter the current value of your investment, along with the current date.**

Calculation of XIRR with first purchase

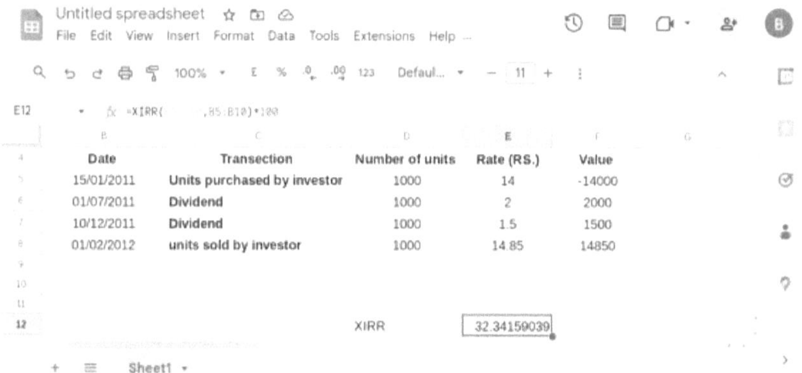

Date	Transection	Number of units	Rate (RS.)	Value
15/01/2011	Units purchased by investor	1000	14	-14000
01/07/2011	Dividend	1000	2	2000
10/12/2011	Dividend	1000	1.5	1500
01/02/2012	units sold by investor	1000	14.85	14850
	XIRR			32.34159039

Calculation of XIRR with additional purchase

Date	Transection	Number of units	Rate (RS.)	Value
15/01/2011	Units purchased by investor	1000	14	-14000
01/07/2011	Dividend	1000	2	2000
15/09/2011	Additional units purchased by investor	500	13	-6500
10/12/2011	Dividend	1500	1.5	2250
01/02/2012	Units sold by investor	1000	14.85	14850
01/02/2012	units rerained by investor	500	14.85	7425
	XIRR		38.57818581	

Compound annual growth rate, or CAGR, is the mean annual growth rate of an investment over a specified period of time longer than one year. It represents one of the most accurate ways to calculate and determine returns for individual assets, investment portfolios, and anything that can rise or fall in value over time.

CAGR in Excel Using Dates

$$CAGR = \left(\frac{End\ Value}{Start\ Value} \right)^{\left(\frac{365}{Days} \right)} - 1$$

CAGR= (Ending value/Beginning value)^(1/n) -1

The CAGR is calculated by:

- Dividing the value of an investment at the end of a period by its value at the beginning of that period

- Raising the result to an exponent of one divided by the number of years

- Subtracting one from the subsequent result

- Multiplying by 100 to convert the answer into a percentage

CAGR, or Compound Annual Growth Rate, works by calculating the average annual growth rate of an investment over a specific period, assuming that the growth is compounded.

Let's understand how CAGR works with an illustration:

CAGR calculates an investment's average annual growth rate over a specific period, considering compounding. Let's consider an investment with a starting value of Rs 100,000, and it grew to Rs 155,000 at the end of eleven years.

To calculate CAGR, we use the formula: CAGR = (Ending Value / Beginning Value)^(1 / Number of Years) – 1.

Using the formula, we calculated the CAGR for this investment = 4.48%

This means that, on average, the investment grew by approximately 4.48% per year over the eleven-year period.

The below graph shows how CAGR smooths out these fluctuations and gives you a single rate of growth that you can use for comparison purposes. On the other hand, the annualized returns show the investment's performance every year.

How to Calculate Compound Annual Growth Rate (CAGR)

To calculate the Compound Annual Growth Rate (CAGR), follow these steps:

    a) Determine the starting value (the initial investment or any other value you are measuring) and the ending value (the value at the end of the specified period).

    b) Calculate the total number of years or periods over which the growth occurred.

    c) *Use the formula: CAGR = (Ending Value / Starting Value)^(1 / Number of Years) – 1.*

    Multiply the result by 100 to express the CAGR as a percentage.

Here's an example to illustrate the calculation:

Let's say you invested Rs 10,000 in any mutual fund and after 5 years, it grew to Rs 15,000.

Starting Value: Rs 10,000

Ending Value: Rs 15,000

Number of Years: 5

CAGR = (Rs 15,000 / Rs 10,000)^(1 / 5) – 1

CAGR = 0.08447 or 8.45%

The CAGR in this case is approximately 8.45%, indicating that the investment grew by an average of 8.45% annually over the 5-year period.

Why is CAGR useful to you

Generally, people tend to look at returns in absolute terms. Imagine you have invested ₹1000 in a particular mutual fund for a period of three years. At the end of the third year, the value of your investment grew to ₹1,850. In absolute terms, your fund has generated a return of 85% over the three years. You could say that your money has nearly doubled during this period.

However, this can be a bit misleading. It does not tell you how much your investment has grown each year. This is where CAGR becomes very useful.

Here, let's calculate the CAGR to understand its benefits.

CAGR = [(1850/1000)^(1/3)] – 1

OR

CAGR = 23%

In other words, your investment in the fund has given you an average return of 23% every year over the last three years.

Essentially, CAGR lets you know the compounded returns you earn on an annual basis irrespective of the individual yearly performances of the fund.

This is because your investments do not grow at the same rate every year. In some years, you may have high returns while during other years, your returns may be lower. In fact, it is possible to earn negative returns too.

CAGR provides you with information on the average returns earned by a fund every year in a certain time period. This is not a true rate of return. Rather, it is a representational figure of how much your investment growth provided they grew at the same rate every year.

Use of CAGR

There are multiple uses for Compound Annual Growth Rate (CAGR).

1) Performance comparison:

CAGR provides a standardised measure to compare performance of different investments over a specific period. It allows investors to evaluate investments equally, considering the average annual growth rate rather than absolute numbers.

2) *Long-term planning:*

CAGR helps in long-term investment planning by estimating the potential growth of an investment over time. It allows investors to project the future value of their investments and make informed decisions based on the expected average annual growth rate.

3) *Risk assessment:*

CAGR can help assess the risk associated with an investment. If the CAGR of an investment is consistently positive over a long period, it indicates a more stable and reliable growth pattern, which may be attractive to risk-averse investors.

4) *Performance evaluation:*

CAGR enables investors to evaluate the historical performance

of their investments. By comparing the CAGR of their investments against benchmark indices or industry standards, investors can gauge their investment strategies' effectiveness and identify improvement areas.

Modified Duration

Modified duration measures the change in the value of a bond in response to a change in 100-basis-point (1%) change in interest rates. The term modified duration is based on the concept that security prices and interest rates are inversely related. *It measures the sensitivity of bond price to the interest rates.*

While maturity influences the price risk in a debt security, a more scientific approach would be modified duration.

Suppose thee modified duration is to be calculated as of January 15, 2012, for a security of 11% p.a., payable half-yearly, until it matures on January 25, 2014. The security is currently traded in the market at a yield of 11.5%.

The modified duration can be *calculated using the MDURATION function in Spreadsheet.*

Advantages of modified duration

a) Duration allows bonds of different maturities and coupon rates to be compared. This makes decision making regarding bond finance easier and more effective.

b) If a portfolio of bonds is constructed based on weighted average duration, it is possible to identify the change in value of the portfolio as interest rates change.

Table1 copy XLSX

File Edit View Insert Format Data Tools Help Accessibility

100% £ % 123 Arial 10 B I A

D12 =MDURATION(D3,D5,D6,D8,D10)

	A	B	C	D	E	F	G
1							
2							
3		Settlement Date		15/01/2012			
4							
5		Maturity Date		25/01/2014			
6		Copoun		11%			
7							
8		Yield		11.50%			
9							
10		Frequency		2			
11							
12		Modified Duration		1.682128224			
13							
14							
15							

Limitations of modified duration?

a) Modified Durations are more commonly used than Macaulay Durations, but they both suffer from the same limitations.

b) Modified Durations are more sensitive to changes in interest rates, making them useful in predicting short-term price changes, but they can be less accurate in predicting long-term price changes.

The implication is that if the yield in the market were to change by 1%, this debt security is likely to change in value by 1.68%

If the coupon payments are quarterly then frequency will be 4

If the coupon payments are semi-annually then frequency will be 2

If the coupon payments are annually then frequency will be 1

Beta

In investing, _beta is a statistical measure of how volatile a security's returns are relative to the market as a whole._ It's a component of the Capital Asset Pricing Model (CAPM) and is often represented by the Greek letter β.

Beta can help investors _decide whether to invest in a riskier stock that's highly correlated with the market (beta above 1), or a less volatile one (beta below 1)._

For example, a beta of 1.3 suggests that the stock is 30% more volatile than the market.

Beta is less useful for investors who want to predict future movements in prices because it's calculated using historical market data. Beta also measures past performance and does not guarantee future returns. It's less effective over long periods since the risk level of an asset can change drastically over the years.

The beta coefficient can be interpreted as follows:

- **$\beta = 1$: Exactly as volatile as the market**
- **$\beta > 1$: More volatile than the market**
- **$\beta < 1$: Less volatile than the market**
- **$\beta = 0$: Uncorrelated to the market**
- **$\beta < 0$: Negatively correlated to the market**

High beta stocks make portfolios riskier but increase the chance of higher returns. More risk-averse investors might shy away from high-beta stocks, while more aggressive investors might be more inclined to chase them.

We saw that there are two risks in investing in equity:

a) **Systematic Risk** is inherent to equity investments, for example, the risk arising out of political turbulence, inflation etc. It would affect all equities, and therefore cannot be avoided.

b) **Non-systematic Risk** is unique to a company, for example, risk that a key pharma compound will not be approved, or the risk that a high performing CEO leaves the company. Non-systematic risk can be minimised by holding a diversified portfolio of investments.

Since investors can diversify away their non-systematic risks, they have to be compensated only for systematic risk.

Calculation of beta calls for information on the value of the market index on each of the days for which the NAV information is used. A diversified index like CNX Nifty has to be used.

Based on the value of Nifty on each of those days, the periodic returns can be calculated, as was done for the scheme returns. Thereafter, the 'slope' function can be used in Spreadsheet.

The slope formula (Beta) helps to find out the changes made in scheme return as compared to changes in nifty return

Table1 copy XLSX

File Edit View Insert Format Data Tools Extensions Help Accessibility

100% | $ % .0 .00 123 | Verdana | − 10 + | B I | A

C18 | fx =Slope(F3:F14, D3:D14)

	A	B	C	D	E	F	G	H
1		Date	NAV	Periodic Scheme Return	Nifty	Periodic Nifty Return		
2		15-Jan-11	13.50		5000			
3		15-Feb-11	13.75	1.85%	5100	2.00%		
4		15-Mar-11	13.50	-1.82%	5010	-1.76%		
5		15-Apr-11	13.60	0.74%	5050	0.80%		
6		15-May-11	13.65	0.37%	5070	0.40%		
7		15-Jun-11	13.75	0.73%	5100	0.59%		
8		15-Jul-11	13.25	-3.64%	4900	-3.92%		
9		15-Aug-11	13.00	-1.89%	4810	-1.84%		
10		15-Sep-11	13.40	3.08%	4960	3.12%		
11		15-Oct-11	13.75	2.61%	5090	2.62%		
12		15-Nov-11	14.00	1.82%	5180	1.77%		
13		15-Dec-11	14.50	3.57%	5360	3.47%		
14		15-Jan-12	15.25	5.17%	5640	5.22%		
15								
16								
17								
18		Beta	0.9978599953					
19								
20								

The beta is 0.99 close to 1. This means that the scheme returns are closely aligned with that of nifty

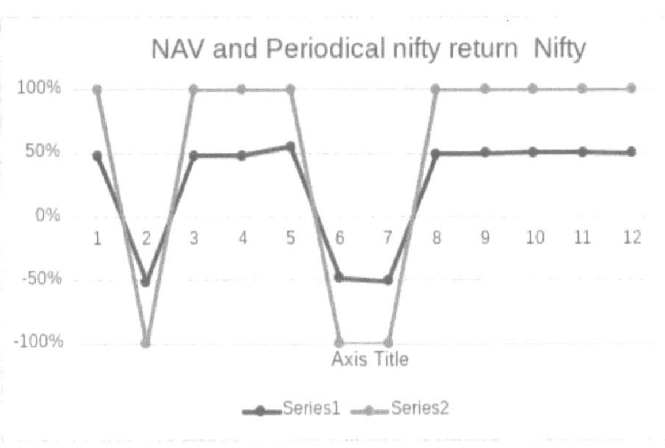

If the beta is more than 1 it means that scheme is riskier than market. A value of beta that is less than 1 would mean that the scheme is less risky than the market

Weighted Average maturity

WAM is calculated by **weighting each bond's time to maturity by the size of the holding**. For example, _the weighted average maturity of a bond issue is the sum of the product of the issue price of each maturity of the bond issue multiplied by the number of years from the closing until that maturity date._ This is then divided by the issue price of the entire bond issue.

Portfolios with longer WAMs are generally more sensitive to changes in interest rates. For example, when interest rates rise, the percentage fall in the value of the longest term bond (e.g. a 20-year bond) will be significantly more than the fall in the value of a 1-year or 5-year bond

Fixed rate debt instruments have a price risk. ___When interest rate in the market go up, the debt instrument already issued, based on lower interest rate will lose their value.___ similarly , when interest rate in the market go down fixed rate of debt instrument gain value

The increase or decrease in the rate of debt instruments because of changes in the market is influenced by the tenor of the instrument. Instrument that have longer maturity are more volatile in response to changes in market yields

In that case Weighted average maturity of the portfolio of the mutual fund scheme becomes an indicator of the scheme's price risk. Higher the maturity, more the rate is likely to fluctuate and vice versa

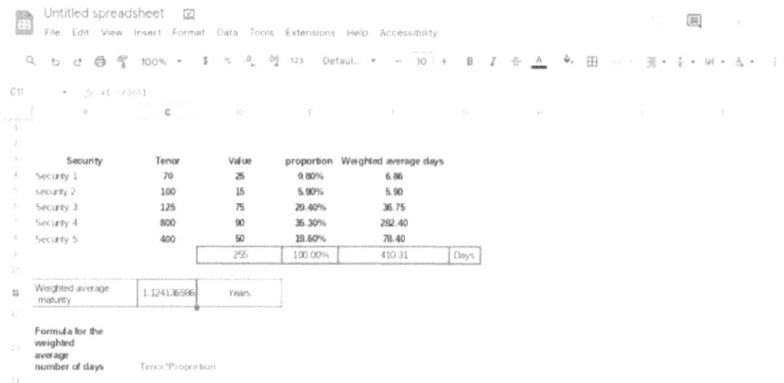

Security	Tenor	Value	proportion	Weighted average days	
Security 1	70	25	9.80%	6.86	
security 2	100	15	5.90%	5.90	
Security 3	125	75	29.40%	36.75	
Security 4	800	90	35.30%	282.40	
Security 5	400	50	19.60%	78.40	
		255	100.00%	410.31	Days

Weighted average maturity	1.124136586	Years

Formula for the weighted average number of days   Tenor*Proportion

By using excel sheet you can calculate the weighted average maturity

Steps

    a) First you should calculate the Proportion

        Formula for calculating the proportion is (value/total value)*100

    b) Calculate the weighted average days =tenor*proportion

    c) Make the total of Weighted average days =410.31 days

    d) Calculate the weighted average maturity = Total weighted average days/365

⏳ Sharpe ratio

The sharpe ratio is a measure of investment performance compared to a risk free asset. It is a ratio of the excess return to the additional unit of risk. A higher sharpe ratio means a higher investment return for the amount of risk

The sharpe ratio is calculated by subtracting the risk free rate of return from the expected rate of return, and then dividing the result by the standard deviation

If sharpe ratio is

Less than 1 —---- Bad

1 to 1.99 —----Adequate/ good

2 to 2.99 —--- Very good

Greater than 3 —----Excellent

A negative Sharpe ratio means risk free or benchmark rate is greater than the portfolio historical or projected return

For example:-

In the example considered, the compounded return was 13.36%. The annualised standard deviation was calculated to be 8.78%

Let us say that a risk-free return of 7% would have been possible, if the same money was invested in government bonds.

Thus, by investing in the scheme, the investor earned a return that was higher by 13.36% minus 7% i.e. 6.36%.

This is his risk premium, a premium earned for the risk taken.

If the risk premium of 6.36% is divided by the standard deviation of 8.78%, we get a value of 0.72, which is the Sharpe Ratio

This indicates that for every unit of risk taken (as measured by standard deviation), the investor earned a return of 0.72%. This is the Sharpe Ratio.

⏳ Sortino Ratio

The Sortino ratio is a risk-adjustment metric used to determine the additional return for each unit of downside risk. It is computed by first finding the difference between an investment's average return rate and the risk-free rate. The result is then divided by the standard deviation of negative returns. Ideally, a high Sortino ratio is preferred, as it indicates that an investor will earn a higher return for each unit of a downside risk.

First lets see how to _**calculate the standard deviation of negative return**_

Dates	NAV	perodic scheme return
15/01/2011	13.5	
15/02/2011	13.75	1.85%
15/03/2011	13.5	-1.82%
15/04/2011	13.6	0.74%
15/05/2011	13.65	0.37%
15/06/2011	13.75	0.73%
15/07/2011	13.25	-3.64%
15/08/2011	13	-1.89%
15/09/2011	13.4	3.08%
15/10/2011	13.75	2.61%
15/11/2011	14	1.82%
15/12/2011	14.5	3.57%
15/01/2012	15.25	5.17%
	1.03116439	

While calculating the negative standard deviation you need to put only negative return cell in formula like in above sheet it is highlighted with green

It is coming 1.03% multiplied by square root of 12

Annualised Standard deviation = 3.57%

The sortino ratio is calculated earlier divided by the annualised downward deviation 6.36%/3.57%=1.78%

- The Sortino ratio is used to determine the risk-adjusted return on investment.

- It is a refinement of the Sharpe ratio but only penalises the returns, which have downside risks.

- To measure the Sortino ratio, start by finding the difference between the weighted mean of return and the risk-free return rate. Next, find the quotient between this difference and the standard deviation of downside risks

Advantages of sortino ratio

1. _**Emphasises downside risk:**_ By focusing solely on downside volatility, the Sortino Ratio provides investors with a more accurate

measure of risk. This is particularly useful for risk-averse investors who prioritise capital preservation.

2. ***Tailored risk assessment:*** The Sortino Ratio considers an investor's specific risk tolerance, allowing them to choose funds that align with their individual investment goals and risk appetite.

3. ***Identifies consistent performers:*** Mutual funds with higher Sortino Ratios tend to have more stable and consistent returns, indicating that they have a better risk-adjusted performance.

Disadvantages of the Sortino Ratio

1. ***Neglects upside potential:*** While the Sortino Ratio is effective at assessing downside risk, it does not consider the upside potential of an investment. Investors who are willing to accept higher levels of risk for potentially higher returns might find this measure limiting.

2. ***Subjectivity in downside deviation:*** The Sortino Ratio relies on the determination of an appropriate threshold for downside deviation. Different thresholds can yield different results, making comparisons between funds somewhat subjective.

Trenyto ratio

The Treynor ratio, also known as the reward-to-volatility ratio, is a performance metric for determining how much excess return was generated for each unit of risk taken on by a portfolio.

Excess return in this sense refers to the return earned above the return that could have been earned in a risk-free investment. Although there is no true risk-free investment, treasury bills are often used to represent the risk-free return in the Treynor ratio.

Risk in the Treynor ratio refers to systematic risk as measured by a portfolio's beta. Beta measures the tendency of a portfolio's return to change in response to changes in return for the overall market.

KEY TAKEAWAYS

- The Treynor ratio is a risk/return measure that allows investors to adjust a portfolio's returns for systematic risk.

- A higher Treynor ratio result means a portfolio is a more suitable investment.

- The Treynor ratio is similar to the Sharpe ratio, although the Sharpe ratio uses a portfolio's standard deviation to adjust the portfolio returns.

The Treynor ratio was developed by Jack Treynor, an American economist who was one of the inventors of the Capital Asset Pricing Model (CAPM).

Advantages of Trenyto ratio

1) *Focuses on Systematic Risk:* One of the key advantages of the Treynor Ratio is that it takes into account the systematic risk of an investment. Systematic risk refers to the portion of an investment's volatility that cannot be diversified away. By considering systematic risk, the *Treynor Ratio* provides a more accurate measure of an investment's performance, as it accounts for the risk that is inherent in the overall market.

For example, let's consider two mutual funds, Fund A and Fund B. Fund A has a higher Treynor Ratio compared to Fund B, indicating that it has generated higher returns for the amount of systematic risk it has taken. This information is valuable for investors who want to assess the risk-adjusted performance of different investment options.

2) *Considers Beta:* The Treynor Ratio incorporates beta, which measures the sensitivity of an investment's returns to changes in the overall market. Beta helps investors understand how volatile an investment is compared to the market as a whole. By including beta in the calculation, the Treynor Ratio provides a measure of an investment's performance relative to its level of risk.

For instance, if a stock has a beta of 1, it is expected to move in line with the market. On the other hand, a stock with a beta greater than 1 is expected to be more volatile than the market. By factoring in beta, the Treynor Ratio enables investors to compare the risk-adjusted returns of different investments, taking into consideration their sensitivity to market movements.

Limitations:

1) *Ignores Unsystematic Risk:* One limitation of the Treynor Ratio is that it does not consider unsystematic risk, also known as idiosyncratic risk. Unsystematic risk refers to the risk that is specific to a particular investment and can be diversified away by holding a well-diversified portfolio. Since the Treynor Ratio only focuses on systematic risk, it may not provide a complete picture of an investment's risk-adjusted performance.

For example, if a mutual fund has a high Treynor Ratio due to its exposure to systematic risk, it may not necessarily indicate superior performance if it is also exposed to high levels of unsystematic risk. Therefore, investors should be cautious when solely relying on the Treynor Ratio and consider other risk measures to assess the overall risk profile of an investment.

2) ***Sensitivity to Market Movements:*** Another limitation of the Treynor Ratio is its sensitivity to market movements. Since the ratio incorporates beta, which measures an investment's sensitivity to market fluctuations, it can be heavily influenced by <u>short-term market</u> trends. This sensitivity may lead to misleading conclusions about an investment's performance, especially during periods of <u>market volatility</u>

For instance, if the market experiences a sudden downturn, the Treynor Ratio of an investment may decrease, even if its underlying fundamentals remain strong. This highlights the importance of considering the limitations of the Treynor Ratio and using it in conjunction with other performance measures to gain a more comprehensive **<u>understanding of an investment's risk-adjusted returns</u>**.

Understanding the Treynor Ratio

The Formula for the Treynor Ratio is:

$$Treynor\ Ratio = \frac{Portfolio\ Return - Risk\ Free\ Rate}{Portfolio\ Beta}$$

For example, assume Portfolio Manager A achieves a <u>portfolio return</u> of 8% in a given year, when the <u>risk-free rate of return</u> is 5%; the portfolio has a beta of 1.5. In the same year,

By applying the formula

Treynor ratio =(8%-5%)/1.5

    = 3%/1.5

    =2.0

Portfolio Manager B achieved a portfolio return of 7%, with a portfolio beta of 0.8.

Treynor ratio =(8%-7%)/0.8

    = 1%/0.8

    =2.5

The Treynor Index is therefore 2.0 for Portfolio Manager A, and 2.5 for Portfolio Manager B. While Portfolio Manager A exceeded Portfolio Manager B's performance by a percentage point, Portfolio Manager B actually had the better performance on a risk-adjusted basis.

Jensen's Alpha

Alpha is a measure of the fund manager's performance.

In the process of managing a non-index scheme, the fund manager may take a risk (as measured by beta) that is different from the market risk; the scheme returns too are likely to be different from the market.

Logically, if the fund manager took a higher risk than the market, he ought to deliver a return that is higher than the market.

Alpha compares the return which ought to have been generated (for the risk taken) by the scheme with the return that was actually generated. The difference between the two is out-performance (if actual return is higher) or under-performance (if actual return is lower).

Alpha can be positive or negative. It is calculated using the INTERCEPT function in Between two fund managers of competing diversified equity schemes, the one with higher alpha is considered to have delivered better risk adjusted returns.

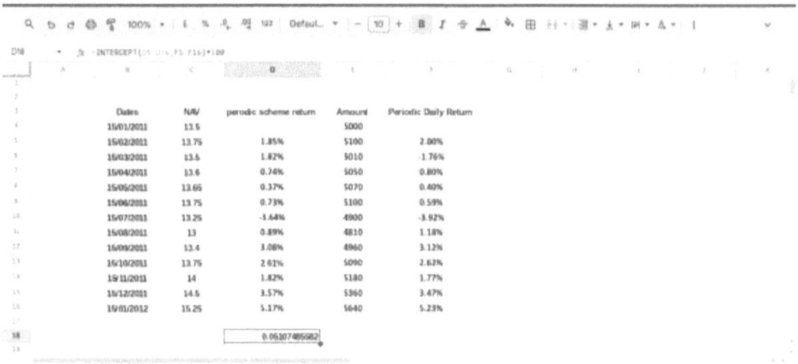

Dates	NAV	periodic scheme return	Amount	Periodic Daily Return
15/01/2011	13.5		5000	
15/02/2011	13.75	1.85%	5100	2.00%
15/03/2011	13.6	1.82%	5010	-1.76%
15/04/2011	13.6	0.74%	5050	0.80%
15/05/2011	13.66	0.37%	5070	0.40%
15/06/2011	13.75	0.73%	5100	0.59%
15/07/2011	13.25	-3.64%	4900	-3.92%
15/08/2011	13	0.89%	4810	1.18%
15/09/2011	13.4	3.08%	4960	3.12%
15/10/2011	13.75	2.61%	5090	2.62%
15/11/2011	14	1.82%	5180	1.77%
15/12/2011	14.5	3.57%	5360	3.47%
15/01/2012	15.25	5.17%	5640	5.23%

0.06107495982

Advantages of Jensen's alpha

- This tool offers insight into a portfolio or investment's performance after factoring in the associated risk level, enabling investors to compare multiple investments having different risk levels.

- As noted above, a positive Jensen's alpha can suggest that a portfolio or financial instrument delivers above-average financial gains considering its risk level, indicating that the strategy could be more effective than the others.

- It can help one determine if a fund manager merely benefits from the overall market trends or adds any value via their investment strategies by isolating the effect of the investment decisions made by a portfolio manager from the market movements.

Disadvantages

- It can be sensitive to the changes taking place in market conditions, making it crucial for an investor to take into account how various market environments may impact the risk-adjusted performance of their portfolio.

- The calculation of Jensen's measure involves using historical data, which may not be indicative of the investment portfolio's future performance.

- This concept's validity depends on the assumptions underlying the capital asset pricing model, for example, the linear relation between expected returns and risk and a risk-free rate's existence.

Jensen's Alpha vs Sharpe Ratio vs Treynor Ratio

The concepts of Sharpe ratio, Treynor ratio, and Jensen's alpha can be confusing, especially for people new to finance. One must know their meaning and learn how they differ to understand how they work. In that regard, individuals must look at their distinct characteristics.

Jensen's Alpha	Sharpe Ratio	Treynor Ratio
This is the measure of the additional return generated by an investment over the market's expected return.	The Sharpe ratio refers to the measurement of a portfolio or an investment's risk-adjusted returns.	It is the risk-adjusted measure of an investment's returns.
Jensen's measure uses historical information.	It involves a forward-looking approach.	Treynor helps in measuring historical performance.
It is based on systematic risk only.	This includes both unsystematic and systematic risk.	It includes only systematic risk.

Frequently Asked Questions (FAQs)

1) What is the difference between alpha and Jensen's alpha?

Ans:- Typically, when looking at investments or portfolios having similar beta ratios, investors or fund managers prefer the one with a higher Jensen's measure. This is because the higher alpha implies better rewards at the same level of financial risk.

2) Is Jensen's Alpha the same as CAPM?

Ans:-No, one must remember that these two concepts are not the same. The CAPM or capital asset pricing model involves measuring the expected returns on any investment on the basis of the risk level associated with it. That said, the difference between the portfolio returns and the CAPM expected return is Jensen's measure.

3) Who developed Jensen's alpha?

Ans:-Michael Jensen developed Jensen's measure in 1968.

4) Is Jensen's alpha the intercept?

Ans:-It is the regression equation's intercept within the capital asset pricing model. Moreover, in effect, it is the additional return adjusted for systematic risk.

Question For Practice (MCQ)

1) _________ financial metric that calculates the rate of return on investments based on their cash flows.

   a) **XIRR**

   b) CAGR

   c) IRR

   d) All of the above

2) IRR is used to calculate _________

   a) **Lumpsum investment**

   b) Single investment

   c) Dividend

   d) Return

3) XIRR is suitable to calculate the performance of investment like __

a) **SIP**

b) SWP

c) Dividend reinvestment

d) Mutual fund

4) CAGR works by calculating the average __________ over a specific period

a) **Annual growth of an investment**

b) Compound growth

c) Annual return on investment

d) Annual dividend on investment

5) __________ provides a standardised measure to compare performance of different investments over a specific period.

a) XIRR

b) IRR

c) **CAGR**

d) Modified duration

6) CAGR helps in _________ planning by estimating the potential growth of an investment over time.

a) Short term investment planning

b) Investment planning

c) **long-term investment**

d) Risk -return

7) If the CAGR of an investment is consistently positive over a long period, it indicates a more stable and reliable growth pattern, which may be attractive to __________

a) **Risk-averse investors.**

b) Risk- taker

c) Risk seeking investor

d) All of the above

8) CAGR enables investors to evaluate the _______ of their investments.

a) Risk taking capacity

b) **Historical performance**

c) Liquidity

d) Return

9) The term modified duration is based on the concept that security prices and interest rates are_________ related

a) **Inversely**

b) Directly

c) Either a or b

d) None of the above

10) While maturity influences the price risk in a debt security, a more scientific approach would be ___________

a) **Modified duration.**

b) XIRR

c) IRR

d) CAGR

11) Modified duration measures the change in the value of a bond in response to a change in change in __________

a) **interest rates.**

b) Market rate

c) Liquidity

d) Return

12) Risk arising out of inflation is called _________

a) credit risk

b) Interest rate risk

c) **Systematic Risk**

d) Non- systematic Risk

13) When the Beta is closed to 1 this means the scheme is ________

a) Risky

b) Not risky

c) **Close to nifty**

d) Equal to nifty

14) ______________ is a statistical measure of how volatile a security's returns are relative to the market as a whole.

a) Modified duration

b) Sortino ratio

c) **Beta**

d) Sharpe ratio

15) If the beta is equal to zero that means ___________

a) **Exactly as volatile as the market**

b) More volatile than the market

c) Less volatile than the market

d) Uncorrelated to the market

16) The increase or decrease in the rate of debt instrument because of changes in market is influenced by ___________

a) **Tenor of instrument.**

b) Return

c) Market rate

d) Short or long term investment

17) The sharpe ratio is a measure of investment performance compared to ___________

a) Risk taking asset

b) **Risk free asset.**

c) Nifty index

d) All of the above

18) The ________ is calculated by subtracting the risk free rate of return from the expected rate of return, and then dividing the result by the ________

a) Sortino ratio , mean

b) Sharpe ratio, weighted average return

c) **Sharpe ratio , standard deviation**

d) Sortino ratio , standard deviation

19) If sharpe ratio is less than 1 then it is called _________

    a) Good

    b) **Bad**

    c) Excellent

    d) Very good

20) A negative Sharpe ratio means risk free or benchmark rate ______ the portfolio historical or projected return

    a) Is less than

    b) Equal to

    c) **Is greater than**

    d) Greater than or equal to

21) _____________ is a risk-adjustment metric used to determine the additional return for each unit of downside risk.

    a) Sortino ratio

    b) **Sharpe ratio**

    c) Trenyto ratio

    d) Jennes apha

22) Sortino ratio is a refinement of the Sharpe ratio but only penalises the returns, which have ___________

    a) Upside risk

    b) Either a or b

    c) **Downside risk**

    d) None of the above

23) _______are often used to represent the risk-free return in the Treynor ratio

    a) **Treasury bills**

    b) Commercial papers

    c) Government bonds

    d) Bills of exchange

24) Risk in the Treynor ratio refers to systematic risk as measured by a portfolio's ____

a) **Beta**

b) Mean

c) Average

d) Weighted average

25) Beta measures the tendency of a portfolio's return to change in response to changes in return for the __________

a) **Overall market**

b) Downsize market

c) Upward market

d) All of the above

26) A higher Treynor ratio result means a portfolio is a

a) More risky investment

b) More risk free investment

c) **More suitable investment.**

d) More unsuitable investment

27) The Treynor ratio was developed by

a) **Jack Treynor**

b) Jensen's alpha

c) Frank A. Sortino

d) William sharpe

28) __________ is a measure of the fund manager's performance.

a) **Alpha**

b) Sortino

c) Sharpe

d) Modified duration

29) Alpha compares the return which ought to have been generated (for the risk taken) by the scheme with _______________

   a) The return that will be generated

   b) **The return that was actually generated**

   c) The return which will be risky

   d) The return that will be risk free

30) If the return in Jensen's alpha is higher that will be called ________

   a) **Out performed**

   b) Underperformed

   c) Not performed

   d) None of the above

Define the following

   a) XIRR

   b) Modified duration

   c) Sortino ratio

   d) Weighted average annuity

   e) Sharpe ratio

   f) Jensen's alpha

   g) CAGR

   h) Standard deviation

Short question

   a) Write the features of XIRR

   b) Write the advantage and disadvantages of XIRR

   c) Explain sortino ratio with two features

   d) Explain the jensens ratio with example

   e) Explain the difference XIRR and CAGR

   f) Write the features of modified durations

   g) Explain the difference between sharpe and sortino ratio

   h) Write the advantages and disadvantages of Jensen's alpha

   i) Write the features of Sharpe ratio

   j) Explain the Treynor ratio with formula and Example

Long question

a) In order to ascertain the risk in your investment, which ratio is suitable for investor and why?

b) Which ratio will help tom assess the excess return you have earned by taking extra unit of risk? Explain with the help of example

c) From the following ratio which will be best ratio as per your investment and why?

    1) Sharpe ratio

    2) Sortino ratio

    3) Treynto ratio

Explain with the help of differentiate between them

d) Explain the formula of modified duration , XIRR with example?

e) If the investor wants to measure how a security value changes in response to interest rate changes, which method will be adopted by him and why?

Sample Question paper 1

General Instructions:

1. Please read the instruction carefully

2. This question paper consist of 24 question in two section – Section A and Section B

3. Section A has objective type question whereas Section B contains Subjective type question

4. **Out of given (6+18=)24 question , a student has to answer (6+11=)17 question in the allotted time of 3 hours**

5. All questions of a particular section must be attempted in the correct order

6) SECTION A –OBJECTIVE TYPE QUESTION (30 MARKS)

I. This section has 06 question

II. There is no negative marking

III. Do as per instruction given

IV. Marks allotted are mentioned against each question/part

7) SECTION B- SUBJECTIVE TYPE QUESTION (30 MARKS)

1) This section contain 18 question

2) A student has to do 11 question

3) Do as per instruction given

4) Marks allotted are mentioned against each question/part

SECTION A: OBJECTIVE TYPE QUESTIONS

Q1. **Answer any 4 out of the given 6 questions on Employability Skills (1 x 4 = 4 marks)**

I.   What is a sentence?   1

    a) A group of ideas that forms a complete paragraph.

    b) A group of words that communicates a complete thought.

    c) A set of rules that we must follow to write correctly.

    d) A set of words that contains all the basic punctuation marks.

II.   How tracking your time helps you?   1

    a) We can stay focussed.

    b) We can show everyone how hard we are working.

    c) We can understand where we are spending our time and manage our time better if needed.

    d) None of the above

III.   _____________ shortcut key is used to create a new document?   1

    a) Ctrl + c

    b) Ctrl + n

    c) Ctrl + m

    d) Ctrl + d

IV.   _____________ refers to a person's experiences, training and education.   1

    a) Opinion

    b) Identity

    c) Values

    d) Background

V. __________means to think of new ideas and come up with 1 ways to make it work in real life.

a) Creativity

b) Innovation

c) Critical thinking

d) None of the above

VI. Which of the following actions would not help a green 1 agriculture sector?

a) Using chemical fertilisers

b) Using organic manure

c) Growing vegetables using vermicompost

d) Buying or selling organic potatoes

Q2. **Answer any 5 out of the given 7 questions (1 x 5 = 5 marks)**

I. ___________ is often the first banking product people use, 1 which owens low interest

a) Saving bank account

b) Money market or liquid fund

c) Fixed deposit with banks

d) Post office saving

II. ___________ defines stock exchange as any body of 1 individuals whether incorporated or not

a) National stock exchange of India Ltd

b) SEBI regulation Act 1956

c) Government of India

d) RBI

III. ____________ represents a contract whereby one party 1 lends money to another on predetermined terms with regards to rate and periodicity of interest

a) Derivative

b) Debt instrument

c) Mutual fund

d) Index

IV.   A __________ is like a bank wherein the deposits are securities   1
        in electronic form

        a) Depositary

        b) Depositary participant

        c) Demat account

        d) Custodian

V.   Define equity shares   1

VI.   ______________ is a contract providing for payment of a sum of   1
        money to the person assured of or following him to the person
        entitled to receive the same

        a) Company fixed deposit

        b) Bonds and debentures

        c) Provident fund

        d) Life insurance policies

VII.   Define bonus shares   1

Q3.   Answer any 6 out of the given 7 questions (1 x 6 = 6 marks)

I.   Securities are generally issued in denomination of Rs. 5, Rs.10   1
        or Rs.100. Thai is known as ______________

        a) Face value of securities

        b) Securities issued at par

        c) Securities issued at premium

        d) Both a and b

II.   __________________ is when a listed company proposes to   1
        issue fresh securities to its existing shareholders as on record
        date

        a) Initial public offer

        b) A follow on public offer

        c) Right issue

        d) A preferential issue

III.   Price band will be decided by the company in consultation   1
with __________

a) Regulatory authority

b) Merchant bankers

c) SEBI

d) Regulatory

IV.   __________ may be defined as finance vehicle that allows   1
an investor to raise capital simultaneously in two or markt
through a global offering

a) GDR

b) ADS

c) FCCB

d) ADR

V.   Define Rematerialisation   1

VI.   Ractified bad delivery pay in and pay out settlement can be   1
done in __________

a) T+8 working days

b) T+2 working days

c) T+6 working days

d) T+9 working days

VII.   Define EX-Dividend   1

Q4   Answer any 5 out of the given 6 questions (1 x 5 = 5 marks)

I.   __________ are the quantity schemes, where investor get   1
benefit upto 1.5lacs under section 80C of the income tax act

a) Equity linked saving scheme

b) Funds of fund

c) Arbitrage funds

d) Multicap fund

II. ____________ is the standard deviation of the difference   1
between daily return of the index and NAV of the scheme

a) Tracking error

b) Beta

c) Alpha

d) Standard error

III. ____________ documents have the details of the scheme   1

a) Mutual fund OD

b) SID

c) SAI

d) Either a or b

IV. Define sectoral fund   1

V. __________ approaches the securities and SEBI which is the   1
market regulator and also the regulator for mutual fund

a) Sponsor

b) Trustee

c) AMC

d) Board of directors

VI. __________ fund will invest simultaneously in the cash and   1
derivative market and take advantage of the price differential
of a stock

a) Arbitrage funds

b) Multi cap fund

c) Quant fund

d) International equities fund

Q5. **Answer any 5 out of the given 6 questions (1 x 5 = 5 marks)**

I. The tenor period of sovereign gold bonds will be period of   1
________ with the exit option from __________ year

a) 4 year, 2 years

b) 5 years, 1 year

c) 8 years, 5 years

d) 5 years, 4 years

II.   _________ are the mutual fund units which investor buy/sell   1
from the stock exchange, as against a normal mutual fund unit

a) Exchange traded fund

b) ELSS

c) Index ETF

d) REIT

III.   __________are the schemes, where the debt paper has a   1
coupon which keeps changing as per changes in the interset
rate

a) Fixed maturity plan

b) Floating rate scheme

c) Capital protection fund

d) Monthly income plan

IV.   The stress testing should be carried out internally at least on   1

____

a) Monthly basis

b) Yearly basis

c) Semi-annually basis

d) Weekly basis

V.   ___________ handle the investor record of mutual funds   1

a) RTA

b) Trustee

c) Sponsor

d) Board of directors

VI.   As interest rate rises, the NAV of debt mutual fund_______   1

a) Rise

b) Remain in same

c) Fall

d) None of the above

Q6. **Answer any 5 out of the given 6 questions (1 x 5 = 5 marks)**

I.   Transfer of funds from one mutual fund scheme to another at regular interval is referred to as _______   1

    a) Systematic Investment plan

    b) Systematic withdrawal plan

    c) Systematic Transfer plan

    d) All of the above

II.   _____________ promotes the interest of the mutual fund and unit holders and interact with regulators   1

    a) SEBI

    b) Government Regulator

    c) AMFI

    d) RBI

III.   _________ will result cash outflow from the scheme   1

    a) Dividend Reinvestment option

    b) Dividend payout option

    c) Growth option

    d) None of the above

IV.   Define sharpe ratio   1

V.   Which of the following method is used to measure risk on portfolio   1

    a) Standard deviation

    b) Beta

    c) Weighted average Annuity

    d) All of the above

VI.   Which scheme will calculate the STDEV   1

    a) Equity scheme

    b) Debt scheme

    c) Both a and b

    d) None of the above

Answer any 3 out of the given 5 questions on Employability Skills (2 x 3 = 6 marks) Answer each question in 20 – 30 words.

Q7.   Explain the two communication styles   2

Q8.   Explain the default toolbar present on the display screen of   2
        word processor

Q9.   Explain the importance of planning   2

Q10.   Who are the stakeholders in green economy?   2

Q11.   What are the qualities of self motivated person ?   2

Answer any 3 out of the given 5 questions in 20 – 30 words each (2 x 3 = 6 marks)

Q12.   Write a short note on weighted Average maturity   2

Q13.   Why does the security market need regulator   2

Q14.   What is role of stock exchange in buying and selling of shares   2

Q15.   What is the difference between ELSS and funds of fund   2
        scheme

Q16.   Explain the role of the compounding and discounting   2

Answer any 2 out of the given 3 questions in 30– 50 words each (3 x 2 = 6 marks)

Q17.   How you will calculate the XIRR ? explain with example   3

Q18.   What are the differant scheme offered by mutual fund?   3

Q19.   How do you value securities   3

        Answer any 3 out of the given 5 questions in 50– 80 words
        each (4 x 3 = 12 marks)

Q20.   A weakness of XIRR function is that it assumes that dividend   4
        receipts would have been reinvested at the same rate

        According to you, which method was adopted to get rid of the
        above method? Explain with example

Q21.   What do's and don't should an investor bear in mind when   4
        investing in stock market ?

Q22.   Identify from the following (long term/short term investment)   4

        a) Saving bank account

        b) Money market or liquid

        c) Public provident fund

        d) Company fixed deposit

        If you are initial investor which investment you will choose
        and why

Q23.   What are the salient features of liquid funds? What is the   4
       minimum and maximum maturity period of debt paper?

Q24.   Choosing between dividend payout and dividend   4
       reinvestment and growth option- which one is better for the
       investor? Justify your answer

Answer Key

**Q1.   Answer any 4 out of the given 6 questions on   MS   TM
        Employability Skills (1 x 4 = 4 marks)**

I.   a) A group of words that communicates a complete   1
       thought.

II.   b) We can understand where we are spending our   1
       time and manage our time better if needed.

III.   b) Ctrl + n   1

IV.   d) Background   1

V.   b) Innovation   1

VI.   a) Using chemical Fertilisers   1

Q2.   Answer any 5 out of the given 7 questions

(1 x 5 = 5 marks)

I.   a) Saving Bank Account   1

II.   b) SEBI Regulation Act 1956   1

III.   b) Debt instrument   1

IV.   a) Depositary   1

V.   Define equity shares   1

Ans:- Equity shares are long-term financing sources for
       any company. These shares are issued to the general
       public and are non-redeemable in nature. Investors
       in such shares hold the right to vote, share profits
       and claim assets of a company.

VI.   d) life insurance policies   1

VII.   Define bonus shares   1

Ans:- Bonus shares are additional shares that a company
       gives to its existing shareholders at no extra cost.

Q3.   Answer any 6 out of the given 7 questions (1 x 6 = 6 marks)

I.   d) Both a and b   1

II.   c) Right issue   1

III.	b) Merchant bankers	1
IV.	a) GDR	1
V.	Define Re-materialization	1

Re-materialization refers to converting the electronic form of security into physical form

| VI. | d) T+6 working days | 1 |
| VII. | Define EX-Dividend date | 1 |

Ans:- The ex-dividend date is the first day a stock trades without the value of its next dividend payment.

Q4   Answer any 5 out of the given 6 questions (1 x 5 = 5 marks)

I.	a) Equity linked saving scheme	1
II.	a) Tracking error	1
III.	b) SID	1
IV.	Define Sectoral fund	1

Ans:- A Sectoral fund is a type of security that invest in one type of industry or sector like agricultural sector infrastructural sector etc.

| V. | a) Sponsor | 1 |
| VI. | a) Arbitrage funds | 1 |

Q5.   Answer any 5 out of the given 6 questions (1 x 5 = 5 marks)

I.	c) 8 years, 5 years	1
II.	a) Exchange traded fund	1
III.	b) Floating rate scheme	1
IV.	a) Monthly basis	1
V.	a) RTA	1
VI.	c) Fall	1

Q6.   Answer any 5 out of the given 6 questions (1 x 5 = 5 marks)

I.	c) Systematic Transfer plan	1
II.	c) AMFI	1
III.	a) Dividend Reinvestment option	1

IV.   Define Sharpe ratio   1

Ans:-   In finance, the Sharpe ratio (also known as the Sharpe index, the Sharpe measure, and the reward-to-variability ratio) measures the performance of an investment such as a security or portfolio compared to a risk-free asset, after adjusting for its risk.

V.   d) All   1

VI.   None of the above   1

Answer any 3 out of the given 5 questions on Employability Skills (2 x 3 = 6 marks) Answer each question in 20 – 30 words.

Q7.   Explain the two communication styles   2

Ans:-   1) **Aggressive:** Not caring about others views or needs • Dismissing, ignoring or insulting others .Shouting, using strong language, and not listening to others.   1

     Results in Ill-feeling, anger, breakdown of communication

     2) **Assertive:** Expressing yourself while listening to others point, Understanding others views and problems, Disagreeing or saying 'no' without hurting others. Effective communication • You are able to understand others much better and they too can understand you   1

Q8.   Explain the default toolbar present on the display screen of word processor   2

Ans:-

The toolbar is present just below the menu bar and has icons that directly run the command without going through the menu. There are many toolbars but two are displayed by default, the first is the Standard Toolbar and just below this is the Formatting Toolbar. The Standard Toolbar has commands to create a new file, save a file, print a file, insert a table, etc. The Formatting Toolbar has commands to change the style of the text, font size, paragraph alignment, etc.   2

Q9.   Explain the importance of planning   2

Ans:- 1) **Estimating the money required to be spent:** Once   1
       the entrepreneur knows what product to sell and
       whom to sell it to, the next step is to estimate how
       much money will be required to start the business.
       Without an estimate of how much money is required,
       an entrepreneur might invest too much money, or
       may start the business without enough money to run
       the business.

       2) **Estimating quantity of material required:**   1
       Knowing how much material is required helps an
       entrepreneur decide the cost of making each product
       or cost of delivering the service.

Q10.   Who are the stakeholders in green economy   2

Ans:- 1) **Government**   1

       Governments and local authorities make and
       implement sustainable development laws, policies,
       strategies, standards, programs, agreements with
       other countries and actions.

       2) **Non-Governmental Organizations (NGOs).**   1
       Many individual social workers and NGOs help the
       government and society in implementing actions
       required for a green economy

Q11.   What are the qualities of self-motivated person?   2

Ans:- Qualities of Self-motivated People There are some
       qualities that can be seen in self-motivated people.

       a) These are know what they want from life

       b) They are focused

       c) They know what is important are dedicated to
       fulfill their dreams

Answer any 3 out of the given 5 questions in 20 – 30 words each (2 x 3 = 6 marks)

Q12. Write a short note on weighted Average maturity? 2

Ans:- Fixed rate debt instruments have a price risk. When interest rates in the market go up, the debt instruments already issued, based on the erstwhile lower interest rates, lose value. Similarly, when interest rates in the market go down fixed rate debt instruments gain value

The extent of such depreciation or appreciation of fixed rate debt instruments in response to changes in yields in the market, is influenced by the tenor of the instruments. Instruments that have a longer maturity are more volatile than those with shorter maturity.

Therefore, the weighted average maturity of the portfolio of a Mutual Fund scheme becomes an indicator of the scheme's price risk. Higher the weighted average maturity, more the scheme's NAV is likely to fluctuate

in response to changes in market yields

Q13. Why does the security market need a regulator? 2

Ans:- The absence of conditions of perfect competition in the securities markets makes the role of the Regulator extremely important. The regulator ensures that the market participants behave in a desired manner so that the securities market continues to be a major source of finance for corporate and government and the interests of investors are protected.

Q14.   What is the role of the stock exchange in buying and   2
        selling of shares?

Ans:-   The stock exchanges in India, under the overall
        supervision of the regulatory authority, the
        Securities and Exchange Board of India (SEBI),
        provide a trading platform, where buyers and
        sellers can meet to transact in securities. The trading
        platform provided by NSE is an electronic one and
        there is no need for buyers and sellers to meet at a
        physical location to trade. They can trade through
        the computerised trading screens available with the
        NSE trading members or the internet based trading
        facility provided by the trading members of NSE.

Q15.   What is the difference between ELSS and funds of   2
        fund scheme?
Ans:-

1) ELSS   1

Equity Linked Savings Schemes (ELSS) are equity
schemes, where investors get tax benefit up to Rs.1.5
lacs under section 80C of the Income Tax Act. These
are open ended schemes but have a lock in period
of 3 years. These schemes serve the dual purpose
of equity investing as well as tax planning for the
investor. However it must be noted that investors
cannot, under any circumstances, get their money
back before 3 years from the date of investment.

2) Fund of Funds

These are funds which do not directly invest in   1
stocks and shares but invest in units of other mutual
funds which in their opinion will perform well and
give high returns. Almost all mutual funds offer
fund of funds schemes. Let us now look at the
internal workings of an equity fund and what must
an investor know to make an informed decision.

Q16.   Explain the difference between compounding and discounting?   2

Ans:-

points	Compounding	Discounting	
1) Meaning	The process of calculating future values of an investment or loan based on the compound interest.	The process of calculating present values of future cash flows based on the time value of money.	½
2) calculations	Future value is calculated by adding interest to the principal amount over multiple periods.	Present value is calculated by discounting future cash flows back to their present value using a predetermined rate.	½
3) Time orientation	Future-oriented calculation.	Present-oriented calculation.	½
4) Formula	Future Value (FV) = P(1 + r/n)^(nt)	Present Value (PV) = FV / (1 + r/n)^(nt)	½

Answer any 2 out of the given 3 questions in 30– 50 words each (3 x 2 = 6 marks)

Q17.   How you will calculate the XIRR? explain with example   3

Ans:-   Dividend payments in a scheme depend on profits. Some debt schemes do declare dividend daily or weekly.   1½

These are exceptions to the general rule that unlike debt, Mutual Funds cannot work with pre-specified dividend payment dates.

Calculating returns with irregular dividend payment dates becomes easier using the XIRR function in Spreadsheet (in MS Excel, Open Office etc.).

Calculations of return using XIRR Function

Suppose an investor bought 1,000 units in the dividend payout option of a scheme, on January 15, 2011, when the NAV was Rs.14 per unit. On July 1, 2011 the scheme distributed a dividend of Rs.2 per unit. Another dividend of Rs.1.50 per unit was distributed on December 10, 2011. The investor exited the scheme on February 1, 2012, when the NAV was Rs.15 per unit. The applicable exit load was 1%.

The repurchase price is Rs.15 minus 1% i.e. Rs.14.85 per unit. Having bought the units at Rs.14 per unit, a capital gain of Rs.0.85 per unit is earned. The investor has also received a dividend twice during the investment holding period. The cash flows and compounded return can be calculated as shown in Table 6.1:

(The cash flows are shown from the investor's point of view. Therefore, purchase is shown as negative cash

Tow: dividend and repurchase are positive cash Flows)

Q18. What are the different schemes offered by mutual fund?

Ans:

a) Equity funds - funds that primarily invests in equity shares of companies.

b) Debt funds, which invest in debt instruments such as short and long term bonds, government securities, T-bills, corporate paper, commercial paper, call money etc.

c) Hybrid funds These are funds which invest in debt as well as equity instruments

d) Gold ETF - An exchange traded fund that buys and sells gold.

e) Real estate funds - These funds invest in properties

Q19. How do you value securities   3

Ans:- 1. All money market and debt securities, including 1
           floating rate securities, with residual maturity of
           up to 60 days shall be valued at the weighted
           average price at which they are traded on the
           particular valuation day. When such securities
           are not traded on a particular valuation day they
           shall be valued on amortization basis.

       2. All money market and debt securities, including 1
           floating rate securities, with residual maturity of
           over 60 days shall be valued at weighted average
           price at which they are traded on the particular
           valuation day. When such securities are not
           traded on a particular valuation day they shall
           be valued at benchmark yield/ matrix of spread
           over risk free benchmark yield obtained from
           agency (entrusted for the said purpose by AMFI.

       3. The approach in valuation of non-traded debt 1
           securities is based on the concept of using
           spreads over the benchmark rate to arrive at
           the yields for pricing the non-traded security.
           a. A Risk Free Benchmark Yield is built using
           the government securities as the base. b. A
           Matrix of spreads (based on the credit risk) are
           built for marking up the benchmark yields. c.
           The yields as calculated above are marked up/
           Marked-down for ill-liquidity risk d. The Yields
           so arrived are used to price the portfolio.

**Answer any 3 out of the given 5 questions in 50– 80
words each (4 x 3 = 12 marks)**

Q20.   A weakness of XIRR function is that it assumes that   4
       dividend receipts would have been reinvested at the
       same rate

       According to you, which method was adopted to get
       rid of the above method? Explain with example?

Ans:- IRR is an easy approach to calculating returns.
       Indeed, it is widely used in the market. A weakness of 2
       the XIRR function is that it assumes that the dividend
       receipts would have been re-invested at the same
       XIRR rate. This is a questionable assumption.

SEBI has therefore stipulated that returns should be calculated assuming that the dividends have been re-invested in the same scheme at the Ex-dividend NAV i.e. the NAV after every dividend payment. As will be appreciated, after every dividend payment, the NAV goes down.

The calculation therefore calls for the ex-dividend NAV after each dividend distribution.

Illustration:

Suppose it was Rs.12.50 per unit on July 1, 2011 and Rs.13.594 per unit on December 10, 2011.

On the original 1,000 units, the investor received dividend of Rs.2 per unit i.e. Rs.2000 on July 1, 2011.

Based on reinvestment of dividend, the additional units the investor would have on July 1, 2011 would be Rs.2000+ Rs.12.50 i.e., 160 units.

The second dividend would therefore be received on the original 1,000 units plus the additional 160 units i.e. 1,160 units. At Rs.1.50 per unit, the total dividend amounts to Rs.1740.

The dividend re-investment would yield Rs.1740 Rs.13.594 i.e. 128 new units.

The total units thus becomes 1,160 + 128 i.e. 1,288. At Rs.14.85 per unit, this would be valued at Rs.19127 on February 1, 2012, as compared to the original investment of Rs.14000 on January 15, 2011. The investment holding period is 382 days.

The compounded annual growth rate (CAGR) can be calculated as follows: CAGR = 100 X {(12+11) (1+r))-1 i.e. 100 X ((19,127 +14,000) (365+382)-1 i.e. 34.74%

Q21.   What do's and don't should an investor bear in mind when investing in stock market? (any 4 8)

Ans: a) Ensure that the intermediary (broker/sub-broker) has a valid SEBI registration certificate.

   b) Enter into an agreement with your broker/sub-broker setting out terms and conditions clearly.

c) Ensure that you give all your details in the _Know Your Client 'form.

d) Ensure that you read carefully and understand the contents of the _Risk Disclosure Document and then acknowledge it.

e) Insist on a contract note issued by your broker only, for trades done each day.

f) Ensure that you receive the contract note from your broker within 24 hours of the transaction.

g) Ensure that the contract note contains details such as the broker's name, trade time and number, transaction price, brokerage, service tax, securities transaction tax etc. and is signed by the Authorised Signatory of the broker.

h) To cross check genuineness of the transactions, log in to the NSE website (www.nseindia.com) and go to the _trade verification facility extended by NSE. Issue account payee cheque/demand drafts in the name of your broker only, as it appears on the contract note/SEBI registration certificate of the broker.

i) While delivering shares to your broker to meet your obligations, ensure that the delivery instructions are made only to the designated account of your broker only.

j) Insist on periodical statement of accounts of funds and securities from your broker. Cross check and reconcile your accounts promptly and in case of any discrepancies bring it to the attention of your broker immediately. Please ensure that you receive payments/deliveries from your broker, for the transactions entered by you, within one working day of the payout date.

k) Ensure that you do not undertake deals on behalf of others or trade on your own name and then issue cheque from a family members/ friend's bank accounts.

l) Similarly, the Demat delivery instruction slip should be from your own Demat account, not from any other family members'/friends accounts.

m) Do not sign blank delivery instruction slip(s) while meeting security pay in obligation.

n) No intermediary in the market can accept deposit assuring fixed returns.

o) Hence do not give your money as deposit against assurances of returns.

p) Portfolio Management Services could be offered only by intermediaries having specific approval of SEBI for PMS. Hence, do not part your funds to unauthorized persons for Portfolio Management.

Q22. Identify from the following (long term/short term investment)   4

Ans:-

a) Saving bank account

b) Money market or liquid

c) Public provident fund

d) Company fixed deposit

If you are initial investor which investment you will choose and why

1) **<u>Savings Bank Account</u>** is often the first banking product people use, which offers low interest (4%-6% p.a.), making them only marginally better than fixed deposits.   1

2) **<u>Money Market or Liquid Funds</u>** are a specialized form of mutual funds that invest in extremely short-term fixed income instruments and thereby provide easy liquidity. Unlike most mutual funds, money market funds are primarily oriented towards protecting your capital and then, aim to maximize returns. Money market funds usually yield better returns than savings accounts, but lower than bank fixed deposits.   1

3) **<u>Public Provident Fund:</u>** A long term savings instrument with a maturity of 15 years and interest payable at 8.7% per annum compounded   1

annually. A PPF account can be opened through a nationalized bank at any time during the year and is open all through the year for depositing money. Tax benefits can be availed for the amount invested and interest accrued is tax-free. A withdrawal is permissible every year from the seventh financial year of the date of opening of the account and the amount of withdrawal will be limited to 50% of the balance at credit at the end of the 4th year immediately preceding the year in which the amount is withdrawn or at the end of the preceding year whichever is lower the amount of loan if any.

4) **Company Fixed Deposits:** These are short-term (six months) to medium-term (three to five years) borrowings by companies at a fixed rate of interest which is payable monthly, quarterly, semi-annually or annually. They can also be cumulative fixed deposits where the entire principal along with the interest is paid at the end of the loan period. The rate of interest varies between 8-12% per annum for company FDs. The interest received is after deduction of taxes.

As an initial investor if I wants to invest in any security, I will prefer to go for money market or saving bank deposit for short term or else company fixed deposit or public provident fund for long term

Q23. What are the salient features of liquid fund? What is the minimum and maximum maturity period of debt paper?

Ans:- Debt funds are funds which invest money in debt instruments such as short-term and long-term bonds, government securities, T-bills, corporate paper, commercial paper, call money etc. The fees in debt funds are lower, on average, than equity funds because the overall management costs are lower. The main investing objective of a debt fund is usually preservation of capital and generation of income. Performance against a benchmark is considered to be a secondary consideration. Investments in the equity markets are considered to be fraught with uncertainties and volatility. These factors may have an impact on constant flow of returns. Which is why debt schemes, which are considered to be safer and less volatile have attracted investors.

Debt markets in India are wholesale in nature and hence retail investors generally find it difficult to directly participate in the debt markets. Not many understand the relationship between interest rates and bond prices or difference between Coupon and Yield. Therefore, venturing into debt market investments is not common among investors. Investors can however participate in the debt markets through debt Mutual Funds.

One must understand the salient features of a debt paper to understand the debt market.

1. Debt paper is issued by Government, corporates and financial institutions to meet funding requirements.

2. A debt paper is essentially a contract which says that the borrower is taking some money on loan and after sometime the lender will get the money back as well as some interest on the money lent.

Debt funds are available for all durations - from 1 day (overnight funds) to 7+ years (long duration funds). Therefore, you must choose as per your financial goals and investment horizon. Many investors turn towards debt funds for regular income.

Q24. Choosing between dividend payout and dividend reinvestment and growth option- which one is better for the investor? Justify your answer

Ans:- **a) <u>Dividend Payout Option</u>**

In case an investor chooses a Dividend Payout option, then after 1 year he would Receive Rs.12 as dividend. This results in a cash outflow from the scheme. The impact of this would be that the NAV would fall by Rs. 12 (to Rs.100 after a year. In the growth option the NAV became Rs.112). Here he will not get any more number of units (they remain at 1,000), but will receive Rs.12, 000 118 as dividend (Rs.12 per unit * 1,000 units). Dividend Payout will not give him the benefit of compounding as Rs.12000 would be taken out of the scheme and will not continue to grow like money which is still invested in the scheme.

b) <u>Dividend Reinvestment Option</u>

In case of the Dividend Reinvestment option, the investor chooses to reinvest the dividend in the scheme. So the Rs.12, which he receives as dividend gets invested into the scheme again @ Rs.100? This is because after payment of dividend, the NAV would fall to Rs.100. Thus the investor gets Rs.12000/ Rs.100 = 120 additional units.

Notice here that although the investor has got 120 units more, the NAV has come down to Rs.100. Hence the return in case of all the three options would be the same. It must be noted that for equity schemes there is no Dividend Distribution Tax, however for debt schemes, investors will not get Rs.12 as dividend, but less due to Dividend Distribution Tax. In case of Dividend Reinvestment Option, he will get slightly lesser number of units and not exactly 120 to the extent of Dividend Distribution Tax. In the case of the Dividend Payout option the investor will lose out on the power of compounding from the second year onwards.

<u>General Instructions:</u>

1. Please read the instruction carefully

2. This question paper consist of 24 question in two section – Section A and Section B

3. Section A has objective type question whereas Section B contains Subjective type question

4. **Out of given (6+18=)24 question , a student has to answer (6+11=)17 question in the allotted time of 3 hours**

5. All questions of a particular section must be attempted in the correct order

6. **SECTION A –OBJECTIVE TYPE QUESTION (30 MARKS)**

   i) This section has 06 question

   ii) There is no negative marking

   iii) Do as per instruction given

   iv) Marks allotted are mentioned against each question/part

7. **SECTION B- SUBJECTIVE TYPE QUESTION (30 MARKS)**

   i) This section contain 17 question

   ii) A student has to do 11 question

   iii) Do as per instruction given

   iv) Marks allotted are mentioned against each question/part

Q1. **Answer any 4 out of the given 6 questions on Employability Skills (1 x 4 = 4 marks)**

I. —--------sentence is one independent clause that has a   1
    subject and verb and express a complete thought

   a) Simple

   b) Compound

   c) Complex

   d) Either a and b

II. —---------is the shortcut key for save as option   1

   a) Ctrl +S

   b) Ctrl +S+ shift

   c) Ctrl +S+ALT

   d) Ctrl +ALT +F

III. —----------is the process of developing physically mentally,   1
     emotionally and spiritually

   a) Growth

   b) Helping

   c) Ethical practice

   d) Independence

IV. —---is the key for Entrepreneur success, because one cannot   1
deal with frustrating situation

a) Be flexible

b) Strong work ethics

c) Use imagination

d) None of the above

V. —---------factors are those factors that are internal and innate   1
your personality

a) Action factor

b) Personality factor

c) Environment

d) Either a and b

VI. Which is the absolute phrase from the following   1

a) My best friend, Manan, loves cubic diving

b) We watched Sirius, the brightest star in the sky

c) The semester finished, Karen sold all her textbooks.

d) None of the above

Q2. **Answer any 5 out of the given 7 questions (1 x 5 = 5 marks)**

I. SEBI is regulatory authority in India established under —--   1
----

a) Section 3 of SEBI act of 1992

b) Section 4 of SEBI act of 1993

c) Section 3 of SEBI Act of 1993

d) Section 4 of SEBI Act of 1992

II. —-------bond issued at a discount and repaid at face value   1

a) Zero coupon bond

b) Convertible bond

c) Treasury bills

d) All of the above

III.   Which of the following statements is not true?   1

a) A concerned team will check the interest rate risk parameter

b) Stress test policy is mandatory on all liquid fund and MMMF schemes

c) The parameter used in stress testing policy need to be approved by board of director

d) The stress test should be carried out externally on a yearly basis

IV.   What do you mean by follow on public offering   1

V.   The launch of new scheme is known as —--------   1

a) New fund offer

b) IPO

c) Mutual fund scheme

d) Either a or b

VI.   —---------plan will help the investor to invest amount   1
regularly

a) SIP

b) SWP

c) STP

d) None of the above

VII   How the researcher work with the NAV on periodical   1
intervals

a) Daily

b) Weakly

c) Monthly

d) All of the above

Q3.   Answer any 6 out of the given 7 questions (1 x 6 = 6 marks)

I.   Saving are linked to investment by a variety of intermediaries,   1
through a range of financial products called —-----

a) PPF

b) Insurance

c) Securities

d) Fixed deposit

II.   How is SD calculated?   1

    a) It is calculated on a spreadsheet

    b) It calculates value based periodic returns

    c) Periodical returns needs to be multiplied to the square root of no of periods that represents the year

    d) All of the above

III.   How much dividend distribution tax will be paid in case of Individual or HUF   1

    a) 25%+ cess+ surcharge

    b) 30%+cess+ surcharge

    c) 5%+ cess+surcharge

    d) Exempt from tax

IV.   What do you mean by NAV   1

V.   —--------means a already listed company makes either a fresh issue of securities to the public or an offer for sale to the public through an offer document   1

    a) Initial public offering

    b) A follow on public offering

    c) Right issue

    d) Preference issue

VI.   Suppose an investor invest 250 in bank FD @6% for 2 years then how much money he will receive after 2 years   1

    a) 280.9

    b) 383.25

    c) 284.85

    d) 260.9

VII. For a debt security —--------is the amount repaid to the investor when the bond matures   1

    a) Face value

    b) Par value

    c) Discount value

    d) Market price

Q4. **Answer any 5 out of the given 6 questions (1 x 5 = 5 marks)**

I. —--------is the place where buyer and seller of securities can   1
enter into transaction to purchase and sell of securities

a) SEBI

b) NSE

c) BSE

d) Securities market

II. What do you mean by Systematic withdrawal plan   1

III. Which of the following statement is not true   1

a) Investor do not need to do market study for particular in case of mutual fund

b) In mutual fund investor money is managed by professional fund manager

c) A mutual fund provide wide variety to choose any security

d) Either a or b

IV. For a sound track record an investor should be —-----   1

a) Have a positive net worth in all preceding 3 years

b) Be carrying out the business of financial services for not less than 4 years

c) Both a and b

d) None of the above

V. —--------is contract when one party leads money to another   1
on predetermined basis

a) Share certificate

b) Mutual fund

c) Debt instrument

d) None of the above

VI. Which method is used by market intermediary   1

a) NAV

b) CAGR

c) XIRR

d) Interception

Q5. **Answer any 5 out of the given 6 questions (1 x 5 = 5 marks)**

I.   Which of the following statement is not true   1

a) Regulating the business in stock exchange and other security market

b) Regulating the work of broker and sub-broker

c) Prohibiting the fraudulent and unfair trade practices

d) Guaranteeing that investment in NSE will give give good returns

II.   Face value and coupon of debt paper —-------   1

a) Depends upon market price

b) Always remains equal

c) Never change

d) Face vale is greater than coupon rate

III.   —----------------funds are also known as hybrid funds   1

a) Balanced funds

b) Capital protection fund

c) Gilt fund

d) Mutual fund

IV..   Association of mutual fund incorporated in —----------   1

a) 1955

b) 1956

c) 1999

d) 2000

V.   Define CAGR   1

VI.   On public provident fund the interest is payable at —-------- 1

a) 8.7% compound interest

b) 8.5% compound interest

c) 8.7% simple interest

d) 8.5% simple interest

Q6. **Answer any 5 out of the given 6 questions (1 x 5 = 5 marks)**

I. The bond is eligible for —------purposes   1

a) Tradability

b) SLR

c) Commission

d) All of the above

II. Maximum TER as a percentage of daily net asset if AUM is   1
500 crores is —-------for debt fund

a) 2.25%

b) 2.00%

c) 1.75%

d) 1.50%

III. —---------is a monthly document which all mutual fund   1
have to publish

a) Fund's portfolio

b) Fund fact sheet

c) KYM

d) Auditors report

IV. —--------refers to aggregate valuation of company based on   1
current market price and number of shares issued

a) AUM

b) Total asset

c) Market capitalization

d) Either a or b

V. Define Ex-date?   1

VI. Which ratio must be checked by an investor before finalizing   1
the scheme

a) Expense ratio

b) Debt ratio

c) Current ratio

d) Profit ratio

SECTION B: SUBJECTIVE TYPE QUESTIONS

Answer any 3 out of the given 5 questions on Employability Skills (2 x 3 = 6 marks) Answer each question in 20 – 30 words.

Q7.   What are the factors that influence team building?   2

Q8.   Explain the value of Entrepreneur (Any three)   2

Q9.   Explain the process of applying Border and Background to   2
the table

Q10.   What is difference between complex and compound   2
sentence

Q11.   Explain any two policies initiated by the government for   2
green economy

Answer any 3 out of the given 5 questions in 20 – 30 words each (2 x 3 = 6 mark

Q12.   What is difference between systematic and unsystematic   2
risk

Q13.   What is portfolio churning in liquid funds?   2

Q14.   What are the contents of key information document   2

Q15.   Why CAGR calculation is important?   2

Q16.   What are the benefits of participation in depositary   2

Answer any 2 out of the given 3 questions in 30– 50 words each (3 x 2 = 6 marks)

Q17.   What is procedure for investing in NFO?   3

Q18.   What are the objectives of AMFI?   3

Q19.   How are capital gain taxed?   3

Answer any 3 out of the given 5 questions in 50– 80 words each (4 x 3 = 12 mark

Q20.   What are the products dealt in securities market   4

Q21.   What are the rights and duties of investor?   4

Q22.   "If in a mutual fund scheme 75% fund get invested in equity   4
(international) then that fund will be called Equity Fund
scheme" do you agree with the above statement or nor and
Why?

Q23.   If you are an investor and wanted to opt the indexation   4
benefit in which type of securities they should invest and
why

Q24.   What is difference between AMC and sponsor in mutual   4
fund?

Answer key

<u>General Instructions:</u>

1. Please read the instruction carefully

2. This question paper consist of 24 question in two section – Section A and Section B

3. Section A has objective type question whereas Section B contains Subjective type question

4. **Out of given (6+18=)24 question , a student has to answer (6+11=)17 question in the allotted time of 3 hours**

5. All questions of a particular section must be attempted in the correct order

6. **SECTION A –OBJECTIVE TYPE QUESTION (30 MARKS)**

   i) This section has 06 question

   ii) There is no negative marking

   iii) Do as per instruction given

   iv) Marks allotted are mentioned against each question/part

7. **SECTION B- SUBJECTIVE TYPE QUESTION (30 MARKS)**

   i) This section contain 18 question

   ii) A student has to do 11 question

   iii) Do as per instruction given

   iv) Marks allotted are mentioned against each question/part

Q1. **Answer any 4 out of the given 6 questions on Employability Skills (1 x 4 = 4 marks)**

I. —--------sentence is one independent clause that has a 1 subject and verb and express a complete thought

   a) Simple

   b) Compound

   c) Complex

   d) Either a and b

II.   —--------is the shortcut key for save as option   1

a) Ctrl + S

b) **Ctrl+ S+ shift**

c) Ctrl+ S+ ALT

d) Ctrl+ ALT+F

III.   —---------is the process of developing physically mentally,   1
emotionally and spiritually

a) **Growth**

b) Helping

c) Ethical practice

d) Independence

IV.   —----is the key for Entrepreneur success, because one   1
cannot deal with frustrating situation

a) Be flexible

b) **Strong work ethics**

c) Use imagination

d) None of the above

V.   —---------factors are those factor that are internal and innate   1
your personality

a) Action factor

b) Personality factor

c) Environment

d) **Either a and b**

VI.   Which is the absolute phrase from the following   1

a) **My best friend, Manan, loves cubic diving**

b) We watched Sirius, the brightest star in the sky

c) The semester finished, Karen sold all her textbooks.

d) None of the above

Q2.   Answer any 5 out of the given 7 questions (1 x 5 = 5 marks)

I.   SEBI is regulatory authority in India established under —-----   1

a) **Section 3 of SEBI act of 1992**

b) Section 4 of SEBI act of 1993

c) Section 3 of SEBI Act of 1993

d) Section 4 of SEBI Act of 1992

II.   —-------bond issued at a discount and repaid at face value   1

a) **Zero coupon bond**

b) Convertible bond

c) Treasury bills

d) All of the above

III.   Which of the following statements is not true?   1

a) A concerned team will check the interest rate risk parameter

b) Stress test policy is mandatory on all liquid fund and MMMF schemes

c) The parameter used in stress testing policy need to be approved by board of director

d) **The stress test should be carried out externally on a yearly basis**

IV.   What do you mean by follow on public offering   1

A follow-on public offering (Further Issue) is when an already listed company makes either a fresh issue of securities to the public or an offer for sale to the public, through an offer document.

V.   The launch of new scheme is known as —--------   1

a) **New fund offer**

b) IPO

c) Mutual fund scheme

d) Either a or b

VI.   —----------plan will help the investor to invest amount   1
regularly

a) **SIP**

b) SWP

c) STP

d) None of the above

VII	How the researcher work with the NAV on periodical intervals

a) **Daily**

b) Weakly

c) Monthly

d) All of the above

Q3.	**Answer any 6 out of the given 7 questions (1 x 6 = 6 marks)**
I.	Saving are linked to investment by a variety of intermediaries, through a range of financial products called ——-----

a) PPF

b) Insurance

c) **Securities**

d) Fixed deposit

II.	How is SD calculated?

a) It is calculated on a spreadsheet

b) It calculates value based periodic returns

c) Periodical returns needs to be multiplied to the square root of no of periods that represents the year

d) **All of the above**

III.	How much dividend distribution tax will be paid in case of Individual or HUF

a) **25%+cess+surcharge**

b) 30%+cess+surcharge

c) 5%+cess+surcharge

d) Exempt from tax

IV.	What do you mean by NAV?
Ans.	Net Assets of a scheme is the market value of assets of the scheme less all scheme liabilities. NAV i.e. net asset value is calculated by dividing the value of Net Assets by the outstanding number of Units.

V. —--------means a already listed company makes either a 1
fresh issue of securities to the public or an offer for sale to
the public through an offer document

a) Initial public offering

b) **A follow on public offering**

c) Right issue

d) Preference issue

VI. Suppose a investor invest 250 in bank FD @6% for 2 years 1
then how much money he will receive after 2 years

a) **280.9**

b) 383.25

c) 284.85

d) 260.9

VII. For a debt security —--------is the amount repaid to the 1
investor when the bond matures

a) **Face value**

b) Par value

c) Discount value

d) Market price

Q4. **Answer any 5 out of the given 6 questions (1 x 5 = 5 marks)**

I. —-------is the place where buyer and seller of securities can 1
enter into transaction to purchase and sell of securities

a) SEBI

b) NSE

c) BSE

d) **Securities market**

II. What do you mean by Systematic withdrawal plan 1

Ans. SWP stands for Systematic Withdrawal Plan. Here the
investor invests a lump sum amount and withdraws some
money regularly over a period of time. This results in a
steady income for the investor while at the same time his
principal also gets drawn down gradually.

III.   Which of the following statement is not true   1

a) Investor do not need to do market study for particular in case of mutual fund

b) In mutual fund investor money is managed by professional fund manager

c) A mutual fund provide wide variety to choose any security

d) **None of the above**

IV.   For a sound track record an investor should be — -----   1

a) Have a positive net worth in all preceding 3 years

b) Be carrying out the business of financial services for not less than 4 years

c) **Both a and b**

d) None of the above

V.   — -------is contract when one party leads money to another   1
on predetermined basis

a) Share certificate

b) Mutual fund

c) **Debt instrument**

d) None of the above

VI.   Which method is used by market intermediary   1

a) NAV

b) CAGR

c) **XIRR**

d) Interception

Q5.   Answer any 5 out of the given 6 questions (1 x 5 = 5 marks)

I.   Which of the following statement is not true   1

a) Regulating the business in stock exchange and other security market

b) Regulating the work of broker and sub-broker

c) Prohibiting the fraudulent and unfair trade practices

d) **Guaranteeing that investment in NSE will give give good returns**

II.   Face value and coupon of debt paper ——------   1

a) Depends upon market price

b) Always remains equal

c) **Never change**

d) Face vale is greater than coupon rate

III.   ——------------funds are also known as hybrid funds   1

a) **Balanced funds**

b) Capital protection fund

c) Glit fund

d) Mutual fund

IV..   Association of mutual fund incorporated in ——--------   1

a) **1955**

b) 1956

c) 1999

d) 2000

V.   Define CAGR   1

VI.   On public provident fund the interest is payable at ——-------- 1

a) **8.7% compound interest**

b) 8.5% compound interest

c) 8.7% simple interest

d) 8.5% simple interest

Q6.   Answer any 5 out of the given 6 questions (1 x 5 = 5 marks)

I.   The bond is eligible for ——------purposes   1

a) Tradability

b) SLR

c) Commission

d) **All of the above**

II.   Maximum TER as a percentage of daily net asset if AUM is   1
         500 crores is ——-------for debt fund

a) **2.25%**

b) 2.00%

c) 1.75%

d) 1.50%

III. —---------is a monthly document which all mutual fund 1
have to publish

a) Fund's portfolio

b) **Fund fact sheet**

c) KYM

d) Auditors report

IV. —--------refers to aggregate valuation of company based on 1
current market price and number of shares issued

a) AUM

b) Total asset

c) **Market capitalization**

d) Either a or b

V. Define Ex-date?   1

Ans:- The first day of the no-delivery period is the ex-date. If there is any corporate benefits such as rights, bonus, dividend announced for which book closure/record date is fixed, the buyer of the shares on or after the ex-date will not be eligible for the benefits.

VI. Which ratio must be checked by an investor before 1
finalizing the scheme

a) **Expense ratio**

b) Debt ratio

c) Current ratio

d) Profit ratio

SECTION B: SUBJECTIVE TYPE QUESTIONS

Answer any 3 out of the given 5 questions on Employability Skills (2 x 3 = 6 marks) Answer each question in 20 – 30 words.

Q7. What are the factors that influence team building   2

Ans:- 1) Work Team Structure

It includes goals and objectives, operating guidelines, performance measures, and role specification.

2) Work Team Process

Work team competitiveness and cooperative behavior need to be considered while building a team.

3) Diversity

Diversity influences team building as well as effectiveness. Diversity shall be ensured in gender, background and competencies. Diverse team also ensures creativity.

Q8. Explain the values of Entrepreneur (Any three) 2

Ans:- 1. Personal values for an entrepreneur include passion, honesty, integrity, determination, confidence, wisdom, cooperation, decisiveness, humility etc. These values are reflected in a person's personality and in their perception about certain things. No one really likes to do business with someone who is dismissive, arrogant, egoistic, argumentative and dishonest.

2. Professional values correspond to how an entrepreneur conducts himself or herself in the professional business and workplace environment. Ethics in the business world are also the domain of professional values. Professional values guide entrepreneurs towards being an effective team leader. Some professional values include advancement, balance, authority, leadership, competitiveness, efficiency, opportunity, ethical practice, resourcefulness, excellence etc. These values encourage self-determined action in a professional setting.

3. Social values are values that make entrepreneurs look beyond the core business and have a bigger purpose. These values are what drive entrepreneurs to make the business socially acceptable. In terms of business, social values also influence the objectives of business and the manner in which business matters should be carried out.

Q9. Explain the process of applying Border and Background 2 to the table

Ans:- It combines two independent clauses by using a conjunction like "and." This creates sentences that are more useful than writing many sentences with separate thoughts.

A complex sentence is a sentence that combines one independent clause with at least one dependent clause.

Q10   What is difference between complex and compound   2
Ans:-   sentence

It combines two independent clauses by using a conjunction like "and." This creates sentences that are more useful than writing many sentences with separate thoughts.

A complex sentence is a sentence that combines one independent clause with at least one dependent clause.

Q12.   Explain any two policies initiated by the government for   2
        green economy

1) WILDLIFE PROTECTION ACT, 1972 - The Wildlife Protection Act, 1972 is an Act of the Parliament of India enacted for protection of plants and animal species. Before 1972, India had only five designated national parks. Among other reforms, the Act established schedules of protected plant and animal species; hunting or harvesting these species was largely outlawed. The Act provides for the protection of wild animals, birds and plants; and for matters connected there with or ancillary or incidental thereto. It extends to the whole of India, except the State of Jammu and Kashmir which has its own wildlife act.

2) THE WATER PREVENTION AND CONTROL OF POLLUTION ACT, 1974, amended 1988 - Water (Prevention & Control of Pollution) Act, 1974 is a comprehensive legislation that regulates agencies responsible for checking on water pollution and ambit of pollution control boards both at the centre and states. The Water (Prevention & Control of Pollution) Act, 1974 was adopted by the Indian parliament with the aim of prevention and control of Water Pollution in India. The act was amended in 1988 to clarify the ambiguities and to vest more powers in the Pollution Control Board.

Answer any 3 out of the given 5 questions in 20 – 30 words each (2 x 3 = 6 mark

Q13.   What is difference between systematic and Nonsystematic   2
        risk

Ans:-   1) Systematic Risk:- it is inherent to equity investment, for example, the risk arising out of political turbulence, inflation etc. it would affect all equities , and therefore cannot be avoided

2) Nonsystematic Risk: it is unique to a company, for example, risk that a key pharms compound will not be approved, or the risk that a high performing CEO leaves the company. Non-systematic, risk can be minimized by holding a diversified portfolio of investment

Q14.   What is portfolio churning in liquid funds?   2

Ans:-   A liquid fund will constantly change its portfolio. This is because the paper which it invests in is extremely short term in nature. Regularly some papers would be maturing and the scheme would get the cash back. The fund manager will use this cash to buy new securities and hence the portfolio will keep changing constantly.

As can be understood from this, Liquid Funds will have an extremely high portfolio turnover. Liquid Funds see a lot of inflows and outflows on a daily basis. The very nature of such schemes is that money is parked for an extremely short term. Also, investors opt for options like daily or weekly dividends. All this would mean, the back end activity for a liquid fund must be quite hectic – due to the large sizes of the transactions and also due to the large volumes.

Q15.   What are the contents of key information document   2

Ans.   The Key Information Memorandum (KIM) is a summary of the SID and SAI.

As per SEBI regulations, every application form is to be accompanied by the KIM. The important contents of KIM are:

1. Name of the AMC, mutual fund, Trustee, Fund Manager and scheme

2. Dates of Issue Opening, Issue Closing & Reopening for Sale and Repurchase

3. Plans and Options under the scheme

4. Risk Profile of Scheme

5. Price at which Units are being issued and minimum amount / units for initial purchase, additional purchase and repurchase

6. Benchmark

7. Dividend Policy

8. Performance of scheme and benchmark over last 1 year, 3 years, 5 years and since inception.

9. Loads and expenses

10. Contact information of Registrar for taking up investor grievances

(student can write any 5 or 6)

Q16.   Why CAGR calculation important? 2

For calculating the dividend return we use XIRR method but XIRR does not calculate the dividend if it is got reinvested that drawback is removed in CAGR method (compound annual growth rate)

It will help to calculator the dividend compoundally

Q17.   What are the benefits of participation in depositary? 2

The benefits of participation in a depository are:

1. Immediate transfer of securities

2. No stamp duty on transfer of securities

3. Elimination of risks associated with physical certificates such as bad delivery, fake securities, etc.

4. Reduction in paperwork involved in transfer of securities

5. Reduction in transaction cost

6. Ease of nomination facility

7. Change in address recorded with DP gets registered electronically with all companies in which investor holds securities eliminating the need to correspond with each of them separately

8. Transmission of securities is done directly by the DP eliminating correspondence with companies

9. Convenient method of consolidation of folios/ accounts

10. Holding investments in equity, debt instruments and Government securities in a single account; automatic credit into demat account, of shares, arising out of split/consolidation/merger etc

(Students can write any 5 or 6)

Answer any 2 out of the given 3 questions in 30– 50 words each (3 x 2 = 6 marks)

Q18. What is procedure for investing in NFO? 3

Before investing in mutual funds or NFOs, the investor must have the KYC in place. The mutual funds or the KYC Registration Agencies (KRAs) must be approached to complete the KYC formalities. KYC or know your customer is a form that must be filled giving all details of investor like name, age, address along with supporting documents like PAN Card and address proof.

Once this is done, the investor is to have a bank account and a demat account for transactions in mutual fund units for incoming and outgoing of money and units. Once these formalities are complete, the investor has to fill a form, which is available with the distributor or online. The investor must read the Offer Document (OD) before investing in a mutual fund scheme. In case the investor does not read the OD, he must read the Key Information Memorandum (KIM), which is available with the application form.

Investors have the right to ask for the KIM/ OD from the distributor. Once the form is filled and the cheque is given to the distributor, he forwards both these documents to the RTA. The RTA after capturing all the information from the application form into the system, sends the form to a location where all the forms are stored and the cheque is sent to the bank where the mutual fund has an account. After the cheque is cleared, the RTA then creates units for the investor.

Q19. What are the objectives of AMFI? 3

1) Promote the interests of the mutual funds and unit holders and interact with regulators SEBI/RBI/Govt./ Regulators.

2) To set and maintain ethical, commercial and professional standards in the industry and to recommend and promote best business practices and code of conduct to be followed by members and others engaged in the activities of mutual fund and asset management.

3) To increase public awareness and understanding of the concept and working of mutual funds in the country, to undertake investor awareness programs and to disseminate information on the mutual fund industry.

4) To develop a cadre of well-trained distributors and to implement a program of training and certification for all intermediaries and others engaged in the industry

Q20.   How are capital gain taxed?   3

Funds type	Short term capital gain	Long term capital gain
Equity funds	15%+cess+surcharge	Up to 1 lakh exempt. Any tax above 1 lakh are taxed at 10%+cess+surcharge
Debt funds	Taxed to the investors income tax slab rate	20%+cess & surcharge
Hybrid equity-oriented funds	15%+cess+surcharge	Up to 1 lakh exempt Any gain above 1 lakh are taxed at 10% +cess+surcharge
Hybrid debt oriented funds	Taxed at the investors income tax slab rate	20%+cess+surcharge

Answer any 3 out of the given 5 questions in 50– 80 words each (4 x 3 = 12 mark

Q21.   What are the products dealt in securities market   4

1. Equity Shares: An equity share, commonly referred to as ordinary share, represents the form of fractional ownership in a business venture.

2. Rights Issue/ Rights Shares: The issue of new securities to existing shareholders at a ratio to those already held, at a price. For e.g. a 2:3 rights issue at Rs. 125, would entitle a shareholder to receive 2 shares for every 3 shares held at a price of Rs. 125 per share.

3. Bonus Shares: Shares issued by the companies to their shareholders free of cost based on the number of shares the shareholder owns.

4. Preference shares: Owners of these kind of shares are entitled to a fixed dividend or dividend calculated at a fixed rate to be paid regularly before dividend can be paid in respect of equity share. They also enjoy priority over the equity shareholders in payment of surplus. But in the event of liquidation, their claims rank below the claims of the company's creditors, bondholders/debenture holders.

5. Cumulative Preference Shares: A type of preference shares on which dividend accumulates if remained unpaid. All arrears of preference dividend have to be paid out before paying dividend on equity shares.

6. Cumulative Convertible Preference Shares: A type of preference shares where the dividend payable on the same accumulates, if not paid. After a specified date, these shares will be converted into equity capital of the company.

Q22. What are the rights and duties of an investor?   4

1. Investors are mutual, beneficial and proportional owners of the scheme's assets. The investments are held by the trust in fiduciary capacity (The fiduciary duty is a legal relationship of confidence or trust between two or more parties).

2. In case of dividend declaration, investors have a right to receive the dividend within 30 days of declaration.

3. On redemption requests by investors, the AMC must dispatch the redemption proceeds within 10 working days of the request. In case the AMC fails to do so, it has to pay an interest @ 15%. This rate may change from time to time subject to regulations.

4. In case the investor fails to claim the redemption proceeds immediately, then the applicable NAV depends upon when the investor claims the redemption proceeds.

Q23.   "If in a mutual fund scheme 75% fund get invested in equity (international) then that fund will be called Equity Fund scheme" do you agree with the above statement or nor and Why?   **4**

Ans:-   As per SEBI Regulations, any scheme which has minimum 65% of its average weekly net assets invested in Indian equities, is an equity scheme.

If the mutual fund units of an equity scheme are sold / redeemed / repurchased after 12 months, the profit is exempt.

However if units are sold before 12 months it results in short term capital gain. The investor has to pay 15% as short term capital gains tax.

While exiting the scheme, the investor will have to bear a Securities Transaction Tax (STT) @ 0.001% of the value of selling price.

It is clearly stated that if mutual fund invest 65% in indian equity then only indexation benefit is availed but in above example mutual fund is investing equity that is international that will not be called as Equity fund scheme

Q24.   If you are an investor and wanted to opt the indexation benefit in which type of securities you should invest and why?   **4**

Ans:-   As an investor I would like to opt for equity share in long term because equity share will give you the benefits of indexation even if you are investing for more than 12 months

Tax treatment of Equity funds is –

(In case of long term)

Up to 1 lakh --exempt

.Any tax above 1 lakh are taxed at 10%+cess+surcharge

Financial Markets Management

Final Term – 2023-2024(SET –B)

Class 11th

General Instructions:

1. Please read the instructions carefully.

2. This Question Paper consists of 24 questions in two sections – Section A & Section B.

3. Section A has Objective type questions whereas Section B contains Subjective type questions.

4. All questions of a particular section must be attempted in the correct order.

5. SECTION A - OBJECTIVE TYPE QUESTIONS (30 MARKS):

i. This section has 06 questions.

ii. There is no negative marking.

iii. Do as per the instructions given.

iv. Marks allotted are mentioned against each question/part.

6. SECTION B – SUBJECTIVE TYPE QUESTIONS (30 MARKS):

i. This section contains 18 questions.

ii. A candidate has to do 11 questions.

iii. Do as per the instructions given.

iv. Marks allotted are mentioned against each question/part.

Max. Time: 3 Hours Max. Marks: 60

Q. 1 **Answer any 4 out of the given 6 questions on Employability Skills (1 x 4 = 4 marks)**

i. **Rohan has feelings of emptiness, abandonment and 1 suicide. What type of personality disorder is this?**

a. Borderline

b. Dependent

c. Avoidant

d. Obsessive

ii.   Gregarious, assertive and sociable fall under _____ type   1
        of personality trait.

        a) Agreeableness

        b) Conscientiousness

        c) Extraversion

        d) Openness to experience

iii.   Which type of motivation is associated with activities   1
        that are enjoyable or satisfying in themselves?

iv.   ________ are the individual pages of a presentation.   1

        a. Templates

        b. Thumbprints

        c. Slides

        d. Sheets

v.   What is the shortcut key to underline text in a spreadsheet?   1

vi.   What is the role of Water Quality technician?   1

Q. 2   Answer any 5 out of the given 7 questions (1 x 5 = 5 marks)

i.   What is the meaning of the term "liquidity" in investment?   1

        a) The ease of buying or selling an investment

        b) The potential for high returns

        c) The risk associated with an investment

        d) The time horizon of an investment

ii.   Which of the following is not a Debt instrument?   1

        a) Treasury Bills

        b) Convertible Bonds

        c) Right Shares

        d) Zero Coupon Bond

iii.   Which of the following is the most suitable option for an   1
        investor with low risk appetite?

        a) Junk Bonds

        b) Equities

        c) Fixed Deposits

        d) Derivatives

iv.   **What is an Index?**   **1**

a) A basket of shares

b) An indicator of market movement.

c) An indicator of the economic conditions of the country.

d) All of the above

v.   **What factor/s affects the interest rate?**   **1**

(a) Government borrowings

(b) Supply of money

(c) Inflation rate

(d) All of the above

vi.   **What do you mean by investment?**   **1**

vii.   **Which of the following are not short term investments?**

a) Money market fund

b) Saving account

c) Public Provident fund

d) Fixed deposits

Q. 3   Answer any 6 out of the given 7 questions (1 x 6 = 6 marks)

i.   **__________ is the process by which physical certificates of an investor are converted to an equivalent number of securities in electronic form.**

a) Materialization   **1**

b) Rematerialization

c) Conversion

d) Dematerialization

ii.   **Book Building exercise through the NSE's on-line system offers the following benefits:**

a) A fair, efficient & transparent method for collecting bids using latest electronic systems.

b) Costs involved in the issue are far less than those in a   **1** normal IPO.

c) The system reduces the time taken for completion of the issue process.

d) All of the above

iii. **Demutualisation of stock exchanges refer to __________.**

    a) The legal structure of an exchange whereby the ownership, the management and the trading rights at the exchange are segregated from one another

    b) The legal structure of an exchange whereby the ownership and the management at the exchange are segregated from one another

    c) The legal structure of an exchange whereby the ownership, the management and the trading rights at the exchange vests in one person   **1**

    d) None of the above

iv. **The price band in book building is decided by __________.**

    a) The market regulator

    b) The Stock Exchange   **1**

    c) the issuing company in consultancy with Merchant Bankers

    d) Controller of Capital Issue

v. **The Best Buy order is the order with the _______.**

    a) Highest Buy price

    b) Average Sell price   **1**

    c) Average Buy price

    d) Lowest Sell price

vi. **Stock Split leads to _______.**

    a) No change in market capitalization

    b) Increase in the number of outstanding shares   **1**

    c) Decrease in the face value of the share of the company

    d) All of the above

vii. **Who is a DP**

    a) Branch of Public Sector Bank

    b) Franchise of Private Sector Bank   **1**

    c) Authorized agent or participant of depository

    d) Custodians of the securities

Q. 4   **Answer any 5 out of the given 6 questions (1 x 5 = 5 marks)**

i.   **Key Information Memorandum' is**   1

a) An abridged version of the offer document

b) The memorandum & articles of association the AMC

c) A sheet containing historical NAVs of other fund schemes

d) Annual report of the AMC

ii.   **Physical securities the fund sponsor has to contribute**   1

a) Nothing to the AMC

b) The total net worth of the AMC

c) At least 40% of the AMC's net worth

d) Exactly 50%

iii.   **The custodian of a mutual fund:**   1

a) Is appointed for safekeeping of securities

b) Need not be an entity independent of the sponsors

c) Not required to be registered with SEBI

d) Does not give or receive deliveries of

iv.   **The following do not form a part of the investment**   1
procedure described in an offer document

a) Various plans under the scheme (e.g. Dividend reinvestment plant)

b) Minimum initial (and subsequent)investment

c) Details of who can invest

d) Details of other competing mutual funds

v.   **Better performance than the return on index is given by**   1

a) Passive fund manager

b) An active fund manager

c) All fund managers

d) Non fund manager

vi.   **Which of the following is true about mutual fund?**   1

a) Mutual funds are risk-free investments.

b) Mutual Funds assure fixed returns.

c) In mutual funds the target investors are the High Net worth investors.

d) None of the above

Q. 5   Answer any 5 out of the given 6 questions (1 x 5 = 5 marks)

i.   Risk Free Paper refers to   1

        a) Government Paper

        b) Certificate of Deposit

        c) Commercial Paper

        d) Bank FD

ii.   ___________ Funds are known as passively managed funds   1

        a) Debt

        b) Equity

        c) Growth

        d) Index

iii.   A borrower can default on interest payments   1

        a) Not if he is a known well to the lender

        b) Yes

        c) No

        d) Not if he has promised

iv.   Which of the following is not true about Exchange Traded   1
        Funds (ETF)?

        a) An ETF is like a Bank deposit.

        b) An ETF represents a basket of stocks that reflect an index
           such as the Nifty.

        c) An ETF's price changes throughout the day, fluctuating
           with supply and demand.

        d) By owning an ETF, you get the diversification of an index
           fund plus the flexibility of a stock.

v.   Investors can participate in the debt market through   1

        a) Debt Mutual Funds

        b) Arbitrage Funds

        c) Equity funds

        d) Index Funds

vi. The safer the debt instrument, the ___________ is the rate 1
of interest.

a) Lower

b) Higher

c) Safety of debt instrument will not have any impact on the
interest rate

d) None of the above

Q. 6 **Answer any 5 out of the given 6 questions (1 x 5 = 5 marks)**

i. . …..is a measure of the volatility of a particular fund in 1
comparison to the market as a whole

a. Beta

b. R-squared

c. Standard deviation

d. Alpha

ii. ……………….. measures the dispersion in return. 1

a. Beta

b. R-squared

c. Standard deviation

d. Alpha

iii. **CAGR stands for** ……………….. 1

a. Calculated Annual Growth Rate

b. Compounded Annual Growth Rate

c. Changed Annual Growth Rate

d. Changed Annual Grown Rate

iv. **Which method is used to calculate return with irregular** 1
dividend payment?

a. NAV

b. XIRR

c. CAGR

d. Interception

v. _____________ is a measure of the fund manager's 1
performance.

a. Treynor Ratio

b. Sortino Ratio

c. Sharpe Ratio

d. Jensen's Alpha

vi.   **What is Portfolio Return**   1

SECTION B: SUBJECTIVE TYPE QUESTIONS

Answer any 3 out of the given 5 questions on Employability Skills (2 x 3 = 6 marks) Answer each question in 20 – 30 words

Q. 7	Enlist any four parameters that describe an individual's personality.	2
Q. 8	"Self-Motivation is significant in building one's personality". Comment by giving any two points.	2
Q. 9	Write down the steps to protect your spreadsheet in Calc?	2
Q. 10	What is Eco-Tourism?	2
Q. 11	Explain the concept of 'Electric Vehicle Programme'.	2

Answer any 3 out of the given 5 questions in 20 – 30 words each (2 x 3 = 6 marks)

Q. 12	What are the various short term investments?	2
Q. 13	What do you mean by Buyback of Shares?	2
Q. 14	Write a short note on SID.	2
Q. 15	What are the long term capital gain obligations on equity based mutual funds?	2
Q. 16	Write a short note on absolute return with example.	2

Answer any 2 out of the given 3 questions in 30– 50 words each (3 x 2 = 6 marks)

Q. 17	Write a short note on Investor Protection Fund?	3
Q. 18	Write a short note on tracking Error	3
Q. 19	What is the procedure of investing in Mutual fund	3

Q. 20   What is the main difference between offer of shares through Book Building and offer of shares through normal public issue?   4

Q. 21   What is meant by the terms Growth Stock and Value Stock?   4

Q. 22   What is the difference between ETF and Mutual fund   4

Q. 23   What is the difference between SIP and STP   4

Q. 24   There are four parameters to take a combined view of the Risk and Return for better investment decisions. Give brief of each with suitable statement   4